21ST CENTURY
BUSINESS

21ST CENTURY
BUSINESS

Managing and Working in the New Digital Economy

I.C.C. LIBRARY

JAMES W. CORTADA

FINANCIAL TIMES
Prentice Hall

An Imprint of PEARSON EDUCATION
London • New York • San Francisco • Toronto • Sydney
Tokyo • Singapore • Honk Kong • Cape Town • Madrid •
Paris • Milan • Munich • Amsterdam

CONTENTS

CHAPTER 6 CHOOSING A FUTURE FOR YOUR COMPANY 205

APPENDIX A ON KEEPING CURRENT: A STRATEGY AND SOME USEFUL READING 239

PREFACE

The business climate today is in a state of flux, evolving in many ways, but essentially from the forms familiar to managers and workers during the Second Industrial Revolution into new ones. For sake of convenience, I call the new environment the Information Age, and we work in the New Digital Economy because the Internet has changed so much how we use computers and work. This book is about what tasks both managers and workers in this period of transition from one economic order to another are doing and need to do to be successful. The answer lies largely in doing three things. First, managers have to perform many basic tasks of management essentially unchanged from one decade to another. For example, managers still have to run organizations that generate a profit. Second, both managers and workers need to leverage technologies quickly and effectively and, in the process, adapt to the consequences of such actions. You see this strategy already at work—using the Internet for new channels of distribution of products and services—but the activities required extend far beyond this new merger of computing and telecommunications. Third, most managers and workers have to work effectively in companies (even government agencies) that live in two worlds, that of the old Industrial Age and in the emerging Information Age.

This book is about how to carry out these new requirements. In the early 1990s, an author of a book such as this would have had to defend the notion that things were changing. Today, such an author finds readers very familiar and accepting

the adjective *evolutionary* is a more accurate way of describing what is going on. It is from that perspective of viewing events as evolving that I find answers to the questions about how you can thrive in such a period of change. To be sure, change is more or less intense from one industry to another, and occurs at an uneven pace. Successful managers and workers view their duties as more than just keeping up with the Internet and e-everything. To be successful, the key insight they need is to apply many of the basics of business and managerial practice either in response to changing circumstances or to create those changes, and to do it holistically, thoughtfully, but with a grip on reality.

This book is written for anybody who works today, particularly in highly industrialized (economists would say "advanced") economies. I address my comments to the skilled and experienced employee and to the newly minted MBA who knows her way around the Internet. The senior executive also needs help because he or she worries about the implications of many of the new technologies causing changes in their industry. Middle managers often feel the crush of change earliest in an organization, since they are the ones who normally alter processes, buy and use computers, and experience the consequences of changing market conditions. This book is very much intended to reassure them that the changes underway can be exploited to make their work rational and successful, although their lives will remain fraught with change and churn.

As enterprises increasingly came to share managerial responsibilities with non-managerial employees over the past two decades, it became essential for "empowered" workers to understand and practice the basics of management. As members of teams, as process owners, and as users of an organization's assets, they had, for all intents and purposes, assumed many of the roles and responsibilities of managers. This role is as profound a change as the arrival of the Internet, for instance. There is a melding of manager/non-manager roles, even though traditional command-and-control and hierarchical organizations still exist. Because the roles of managers and non-managers are blending together, yet often simultaneously

institutional knowledge management and personal skills development make sense, and how historical perspective makes it easier for you to see what practices are essential during the transition. I reaffirm the value of process management as a relatively new, yet highly effective, way of organizing work.

Chapter Three discusses the role of knowledge, and knowledge workers, because in a services-centric economy, institutional and personal knowledge is essential to an individual's economic success. Best practices in knowledge management represents a core body of actions people and firms can take to simultaneously exploit the old and new economic realities. I set the issue of knowledge management into the context of such new technological influences as e-business and the Internet.

Chapter Four is devoted to a broad discussion about the nature of work, especially as it is affected by the introduction of the Internet into the daily activities of workers. I argue that the Internet, more than any other current development, is fundamentally altering how work is done. That change is both at the individual task level and in the way organizations organize, allocate, and perform work. It even affects what work is done and by whom. So, understanding the Net, its potential, and the way it is evolving is essential to successful performances by workers and organizations.

Chapter Five looks at how people are hunting for new ways to generate profit, using value and supply chains. If one had to pick the current battlefield upon which the old and new economies are campaigning, this is it. The most important use of the Internet today is in the fundamental redesign of supply chains, because they are being digitized and are the major source of new economic value. The costs of operation are declining and the flow of goods and money is increasing in speed and accuracy. In short, these new supply chains are making it possible to squeeze out inefficiencies, improving productivity while allowing firms to connect in new ways to suppliers and customers.

Chapter Six is all about patterns of behavior among managers and workers that make it possible to live in both the old

still poorly written. My colleagues at IBM have been especially supportive of my work. John K. Condon taught me a great deal about what governments are doing in applying technologies, shattering any image I might have had that public agencies are not progressive. Donald Cotey, Larry Prusak, and Eric Lesser exposed me to the nuts-and-bolts of knowledge management. Ray Lamoureux, one of IBM's key experts on e-business strategies, taught me almost everything I know about the subject, while Harvey Thompson made clear how customers and firms are increasingly coming to interact. Gary Cross went through my discussions about supply chains to make sure that this material reflected exactly what was happening today. A special thanks for encouraging my work goes to Michael Albrecht, Jr., the executive who worries the most about what skills and capabilities IBM's consultants need in the future. Over the past several years, clients, customers, and others have answered questions and tightened up my thinking. They made clear how work is changing, management practices improving, and yet how we are living in a period of transition in which we operate in two worlds at the same time. For the sake of convenience, I simply refer to these worlds as the Industrial Age and the Information Age. I thank them all profoundly for their help.

The team at the *Financial Times* and Prentice Hall have been very supportive. In addition to wanting to publish this book, my editor, Tim Moore, had excellent ideas about how to enhance it. My manuscript improved enormously when Russ Hall scrubbed through every sentence and idea. Moore's production staff did a wonderful job in efficiently moving this book through to publication. I also want to thank Jeff Modjeski at IBM for once again preparing the graphics for one of my books. The views expressed in this book are mine alone, and do not necessarily represent those of IBM, the many individuals who advised me on how to write this book, or of the publisher. Any weaknesses or errors of judgment or fact are my fault, for which I ask for your tolerance. The subject of this book is much like a cathedral under construction in that we have walls up, the roof is being worked on, but it is not yet fully clear what the final building will look like. But you have

INTRODUCTION: WHAT IS THE INFORMATION AGE?

To count is a modern practice, the ancient method was to guess; and when numbers are guessed they are always magnified.

SAMUEL JOHNSON

The term "Information Age" has now been in so much use in recent years that you are expected to know what it means. It conjures up images of people who make their living solely by pushing information about, such as lawyers and teachers, or programmers and stockbrokers. Others argue that what makes today the Information Age is the fact that so many people rely on computers, especially since the advent of the personal computer and the Internet. Sociologists would have us believe that the Information Age is one in which people are networked together through technology and rely on such things as television, radio, and computers with which to conduct their lives, creating a culture different from that which came before it. Economists write that the Information Age is one in which either the computer sector of the economy is massive or the number of office workers doing knowledge work has been growing, providing an economy with more than its Gross Domestic Product. But here are you and I, having to make sense of what the Information Age is about. I describe many of the features of the Information Age in this book, yet I focus only on those elements of the new age that most directly affect businesses.

Complicating our understanding of the Information Age are the changes this age has experienced over the years. Yet a

present some key elements of the "big picture," the economic and social fishbowl in which you and I live and work.

Economists looking at the U.S. situation, beginning in the 1950s, first observed the notion that something was changing. Essentially, what they began and continue to document is how an increased portion of the Gross National Product is being generated by such things as education, computers, media, information, and so forth, and also how the percentage of the work force involved in these activities is growing. While economists debate the numbers, they are nonetheless significant, with some experts today arguing that over 60 percent of the U.S. economy is involved in the creation and use of information as value added activities.[1] The argument goes that a similar process, although less extensive, is evident in other economies, particularly in Western Europe. The rise of the Information Economy—what I prefer to call the New Digital Economy—has been described in many ways, but mainly as a response to the need to control operations of large corporations and government agencies. The argument holds that this need led to the use of more information tools, while proliferation of PCs and the Internet, along with telecommunications, created new economic opportunities. In time, the increased complexity of research and development, products, and use of technology so evident today became a major byproduct of the new era. These are just a few of the explanations.

Toffler and Bell did much to bring the attention of the American and British public to the notion that a new era was upon us in the 1970s with their bestselling books.[2] I will have more to say about their work in Chapter One. However, what a person needs to understand is the observation made by sociologists and economists that there is a direct link between the emergence of an information-centric economy and the expansion of the service sector of the same economy at the expense of the agricultural and industrial sectors. In other words, as a percentage of the total economy of an advanced industrial society, providing services increased regardless of whether or not the economy as a whole grew in size. Again, depending on whose numbers you consult, in the U.S., for instance, the service sector is sometimes recorded as high as 75 to 80 percent

business initiative may be constrained by a lack of sufficient arms and legs to do the work. For another, the evolution to a new age is going on now, so managers have to deal with a spectrum of problems and issues that can be summarized as a combination of living simultaneously in the old (the Industrial Age) and in an emerging one (the Information Age, or more precisely, in the Digital Economy) making it difficult to construct a business model based on one or the other.

This duality of cultures, both economic and social, also plays out in policies and practices of governments rooted in the Industrial Age but trying to figure out when to do things differently in the Information Age. For example, should a government tax goods where they are made and physically sold (Industrial Age thinking) or do you tax transactions consummated on the Internet (Information Age)? Does a government in a highly industrialized country such as Canada, Great Britain, or the United States support free trade and risk low-skilled manufacturing jobs migrating to less developed economies, putting voters out of work in the more advanced nations? What does a policy maker or a government regulator do in countries like France or Japan, where the evolution to service sector economies is picking up steam but the manufacturing sectors are still strong? These are difficult questions, but as every senior executive understands, the answers public officials arrive at have profound implications for the successes and opportunities businesses face.

Besides economic and sociological implications, there is the most obvious feature of the Information Age to deal with: technology. By technology I mean more than simply computers, or even the ubiquitous computer chip, which is popping up in all manner of products and services. I include in this category such things as complex equipment, advanced processes (e.g., modern open-heart surgery), and the knowledge required to use these.

Scientific and engineering knowledge expanded so much and so rapidly in the past century that nothing seems the same. If I had to pick a single driver of change in the Information Age, it would be this combination of newly developed and

straint.[6] The bottom line is that, while technology is unpredictable, it emerges from the creative pursuit of profit.

Of course, as long as there have been economists, sociologists, philosophers, and historians looking at the issue of technology and the emerging Information Age, there has been an intense, sometimes even bitter, debate about the benefits and costs involved. While we have the wonderful historic case study of the American economy of the 1980s and 1990s to point to as a rich, positive example of the economic benefits of the Information Age, economists can also point to the same economy and show that all is not always well. For every Microsoft-like employer that has emerged, there are old manufacturing companies that went out of business. While new information workers were hired, old manufacturing jobs disappeared. The churn in employment and business opportunities shifts and changes in form and content, and often quickly, as we transform eras. That is why, in much of our discussion in the chapters that follow, I address the issue of when to jump off one era and into another.

What economists have learned, however—and this is very relevant for employees today—is that the majority of new jobs created in the second half of the twentieth century in advanced economies occurred when information workers were substituted for traditional noninformation employees in the production of economic value. This is a hard reality, but one that should not be confused during discussions about whether an economy became more or less productive as a result of the introduction of automation or computers.[7]

So what is the Information Age? It is one occupied by people who live and work with a greater reliance on knowledge and technology than ever seen before in the history of the human race. It is an age in which information and technology-based products have economic value, because sufficient amounts of physical goods, shelter, and food exist in advanced economies and make it possible to leverage the new products and services of our times. It is a period in which change, caused by newfound knowledge and novel applications of existing know-how, often dictates economic success or failure.

Rich: The Economic Transformation of the Industrial World (New York: Basic Books, 1986).

7.William J. Baumol, Sue Ann Batey Blackman, and Edward N. Wolff, *Productivity and American Leadership: The Long View* (Cambridge, Mass.: MIT Press, 1989): 158–159.

A NEW WORLD BORN: IT IS MORE THAN JUST TECHNOLOGY

Appearances often are deceiving.

AESOP

The world of work, management, and business is changing. That reality is no longer in question. The real issue is what to do about it. As we move deeper into today's digitized and global economy, we must understand the transition underway, putting it into the context of what we know and will need to do. The successful transition from the old economy of the Second Industrial Revolution to the new economy of the Information Age calls for the careful application of the basics of business, because the fundamental laws of economics and sound management have not been abrogated. Many of the solid business practices advocated by Peter F. Drucker in the 1970s and 1980s, for example, are relevant today as we deal with the changes to many new elements of the economy.

Understanding the context and dynamics of the changes underway makes it possible for both nonmanagement and

must be applied because the sources of profit are changing. That is why managers must understand the informational features of economic activity, the emerging new value propositions (how profits are made), the effects of globalization, and the digitization of so many business activities, all set within the context of emerging political realities. That is why it is helpful to start thinking of our time as a New Digital Age. In short, today's savvy manager must set the table before he or she can feast upon the role of management and work.

FOREMOST AN AGE OF INFORMATION ECONOMICS

During the last three decades of the twentieth century, observers of the business, social, and economic landscape warned that the "advanced nations" of the world were leaving the Industrial Era behind. They were headed into what Daniel Bell called the Post-Industrial Age, one marked by economic activity not rooted in the manufacture of goods. A small army of sociologists, economists, philosophers, and business consultants followed in his path, echoing a similar theme. Those who considered themselves also to be Futurists grabbed headlines with such popular books as *Future Shock*, written by Alvin Toffler, and *Megatrends*, written by John Naisbitt. The trend continued down to the present. For example, Nicholas Negroponte, author of *Being Digital* (New York: Alfred A. Knopf, 1995), provided a well-written, positive, even at times euphoric, vision of a world blessed with the benefits of information technology. However, at the same time we were pummeled with hype about the future, others commented more soberly about the same trends. Those thoughtful observers and effective guides to our future included such experts on business as Peter F. Drucker and Charles Handy.[1] Economic and business circumstances were changing by the early 1970s, yet we were still manufacturing and selling goods, and still eating farm-grown food. Were so many people just wrong about

omy as did the USA. From the perspective of its structure—size and diversity—or viewed simply through the degree of confidence people placed in this country, it was a productive century enriched by the economics of science, technology, and a rising tide of highly trained, well-paid, motivated workers. Despite America's problems, from racism to Vietnam, it is the nation that fed the world, gave it the computer, landed on the moon, and demonstrated benefits of free trade and democracy. As the importance of the computer became evident by the early 1970s, it was most fully developed first in the USA, most rapidly deployed there, and most fully exploited there. And that was only one of many technological "miracles" that "blessed" this nation. Others included antibiotics, high-yield strains of corn and wheat, satellites, PCs, and manned flights to the moon. What a record of success this was for one nation! Hollywood writers could not have written a more compelling story line.

But economists quietly working at their universities looked at events and perceived and told the story in a different way. Beginning in the 1920s, when corporate industrial capitalism finally reached the form it would maintain for the next half dozen decades, the American economy again changed rapidly. Measured by sector, in 1920 manufacturing and agriculture dominated the economy, with services a blip. By 1980, services accounted for more than half of the economy, manufacturing for roughly a fourth of the action, and agriculture less than 10 percent.³ Why and how this happened is a long story outside the scope of this discussion. However, what you do need to recognize is that as the source of jobs and income shifted during the twentieth century away from agriculture and manufacturing and to services, the nature of work did too. The fastest growing piece of the American workforce in this century is the office worker. Economists use such fancy terms as "terciary" to describe this element, while many business writers call them knowledge workers. What happened here is truly revolutionary and profound.

Recently compiled data suggests that the growth in the percentage of the U.S. workforce population made up of knowledge or office workers between 1910 and the end of the

puters around the world. In the 1990s, Europeans and East Asians began acquiring PCs in very significant numbers; large European and Asian corporations had already embraced telecommunications and large system computing for over two decades, also providing innovations in both hardware and software. In short, by the end of the 1990s, computing had become a very familiar aspect of modern work life across the industrialized sections of the world, and to a growing extent in what the World Bank or IMF would term "developing" nations.

Superimposed on the impressive deployment of computing technology today is, of course, the Internet, a technology which caught the U.S. public's eye first, since it was developed in the United States by academics and the Department of Defense during the Cold War. What is particularly remarkable is the intensity of interest and the speed with which this technology became popular with Americans. Their interest ranks right up there at the same level they displayed in the 1920s when automobiles finally became affordable and easy to use. If there is a difference, it is that Americans embraced the Internet faster than the automobile, going from less than one percent having access to it in the early 1990s, to over 35 percent by the end of the decade. In the 1990s a similar yet slightly less intense surge in use of the Internet swept across Europe, East Asia, and to a lesser extent, Latin America and Africa. It became the darling of every "advanced" economy in the world with the partial exception of Japan. Centuries earlier the Cyber Gods had cursed the Japanese with a language difficult for keyboards that come with personal computers, but even in this situation, the Internet became irresistible.

Much about what we have been told concerning the new post-Industrial Age, however, missed one of the most profound changes to occur. Specifically, the change was our growing reliance on information as a source of wealth and income, and more precisely, the extent to which technology-driven firms became sources of new wealth and centers of economic activity. These changes sneaked up on Americans in particular, even though it has had a long run up.[5] Information was never as obvious as a large automobile, as physical and boxy as a TV, or as conspicuous as the hardware of a computer. The com-

was largely resident between his ears, and he probably had limited or no access to any other body of knowledge on his profession. Today, a foreman of ironworkers most likely has a laptop filled with blueprints describing what has to be installed, complete with networking capability to other databases and project plans, possibly to an Intellectual Capital System. If he works for a very large construction firm, e-mail and a cell phone link him to his company, Web sites get him to the Internet and to data belonging to professional organizations. The hidden revolution here is the intrusion of additional information content into otherwise highly traditional jobs. Another quick example illustrates the point. Notice the little radio planted on the shoulders of most police officers in Europe, East Asia, and North America. They are all wired with telecommunications back to a central phone bank where they can get information, communicate what is going on, and obtain assistance. Before a police officer takes action on the street, he or she can routinely ask for additional information that helps, such as whether the person they are dealing with is a dangerous criminal, or has an outstanding arrest warrant.

Both American and West European government agencies that measure features of national economies have only just begun to tell us about the "information economy." They are now publishing task force reports heralding the arrival of this new economy, but they are just barely beginning to reflect that reality in their routine economic data-gathering activities. Their reports on the "information economy" are still sporadic events, occasional, and the subject of press coverage as new news. In addition to not yet institutionalizing the collection of hard economic data on the changing economy is the fact that we still do not have solid agreement among economists or government agencies about what makes up this new sector. In the United States, for example, the government still uses industrial-age industry codes that categorize everything from asbestos manufacturers to zoo keepers.[7] The OECD, one of Western Europe's major economic data reporting agencies, is also very industrial in its perspective about European economics.

Efforts that have been made to redefine work (labor content, assets, and monetary values such as revenues) suggest

some elements of the new economy. While they may seem contradictory or unrelated, they exist in one form or another simultaneously.

Products also have information and services wrapped around them. A quick example illustrates the point. In the 1960s, almost all of IBM's revenues came from the lease of computers and related hardware. At the start of the new millenium, nearly half its revenues came from hardware, the rest came from providing services offered by highly skilled employees. In other words, IBM was generating tens of billions of dollars by renting out their people's brains. Microsoft's stock value is greater than that of General Motors, yet GM has tens of thousands more employees, and mountains of hard assets in the form of automobile parts, factories, and vehicles. In Seattle, home to Microsoft and Boeing (one of the world's largest airplane manufacturers), it is Bill Gates's operation that is now the leading local employer, not the aircraft company. SAP, a highly successful European software firm barely a decade old, is worth more than many well-established and distinguished European firms. The stock of America Online is worth more than that of all the major TV networks in the U.S. put together. Add in the Time Warner merger with AOL, and you have the largest telecommunications/media company in the history of the world. The point is that the creation of wealth and profit is not limited to one country or one industry, let alone to the manufacture of hard goods, nor to such traditional trades as retail and personal services, such as hair stylists or construction. Wealth is being accumulated rapidly, mimicking the patterns of earlier decades when great fortunes were made quickly in railroads, steel, chemicals, telephones, and print media. It is no accident that the richest man in the world—Bill Gates—made his fortune in the information economy, nor that he and two other colleagues at his firm make up three of the four wealthiest individuals in the world, and are soon to be followed or displaced in that ranking by .com founders.

Information economics also affect firms not traditionally thought of as being in the information business. Many North American trucking firms are equipped with onboard PCs that communicate their inventory, status of their delivery efforts,

which made it easier to let patrons know about new books of interest to them. Brick and mortar bookstores scrambled to get online as well. While some have been successful in preserving market share, many smaller firms disappeared, unable to compete, speeding up a process of retail consolidation in that market which had begun in the 1980s.

Utility companies all over the world face tough competition from each other, less because of deregulation than from a firm's ability to use information to compete effectively for a client company's electricity needs. Energy brokers on the "Net" are disrupting traditional patterns of business by bringing customers and suppliers together. Knowledge brokers are appearing in other industries as well. If I want to buy food from a supplier in another state, I don't have to rely on my neighborhood grocery store anymore. These are the kinds of trends and events that make managers very nervous while complicating the life of a consumer. On the other hand, customers are getting more choice and greater value. New business opportunities are emerging and people are making money.

THE SEARCH FOR A NEW VALUE PROPOSITION

Companies like IBM, AT&T, Microsoft, and Cisco live at the crossroads of traditional ways of making profits and are at the point in the economy where many new opportunities and risks exist, created by technology-driven changes in business. Earlier than others, they began to worry about how to run their businesses in this new world. The questions they continue to raise are the same for most corporations, small companies, and even independent business entrepreneurs. Perhaps nothing has caused so much churn and managerial nervousness as the arrival of the capability of doing so much business using telephone networks. You and I think of it as the Internet, with personal computers and telephone lines.

fact that everyone else has access to the network and many are using it. Use it and new things become possible, ignore it and new forms of competition eat at a firm's bottom line. As a result, new rules of commercial engagements are emerging to replace, or sit side by side, with more traditional rules of the game in capitalist economics. Some industries are more affected than others; few are escaping the effects of the Internet. Those with extensive information content or the ability to conduct online transactions are profiting the most and the soonest if they are taking advantage of the new technology.

The second emerging reality is the enormous investments being made in networks and information technology, over and above what is being spent on the Internet. These investments, as measured by percent of a nation's GNP spent on them, are at an all-time high. Within these investments are expenditures for computers and software, telephone systems, wireless communications and their networks, and a mountain of digital devices ranging from PDAs (personal digital assistants) and pagers to personal computers. In the United States, for instance, the percent of GNP spent on IT has been rising at better than two percent per decade. At the end of the 1990s it had reached nearly eight percent, and the number is higher if we include telecommunications.[8] The phenomenon is also present across the world. The result is a global movement to invest in the information infrastructure necessary to convert the hype about a digital world into reality. On a global basis this is well underway. The 16 largest national economies have shown a consistent and increasing percent of GDP expenditures on information technology (IT) throughout the 1990s, from an aggregate of less than one percent to over five percent. This data is for both the U.S. and the 16 nations, but it only reflects IT expenditures and not the costs of end users (such as salaries for those baby-sitting this technology or using it). If anything, the figures understate the true expenditure on information technology. My own research suggests the understatement is off by a good 100 percent. Regardless of the exact numbers, they are big and the trend is clear and obvious. Forecasts for the first few years of the next millennium suggest an upward curve with expenditures doubling within a decade.

that occurred in the late 1990s and beyond. They make it possible for multiple organizations to work together without having to become legal parts of each other, thereby avoiding the complexities and costs of traditional acquisitions and mergers. They make it possible for organizations to come together only for as long as there are sound economic reasons to do so, unlike the more traditional merger or acquisition which is a permanent arrangement—and, thus, a less fluid and a slow way to change. In a value net, the strategic unit is the collection of organizations within it. Those organizations can be many corporations, not simply departments within one enterprise. The benefits of nets seen so far include flexibility, speed in implementation, lower costs of operations, and greater access to markets. Their most important feature: They work.

Lest I mislead you, traditional mergers and acquisitions in the New Digital Economy are still very attractive. In fact, in the 1990s around the world we experienced as big a round of mergers and acquisitions as occurred in any other decade of this last century. Why? Part of the cause is IT. As technology made it possible to manage ever larger enterprises, across bigger tracks of the world's surface, through communications and data handling, it became possible to build ever larger enterprises. In some industries, such as banking, communications, publishing, media, music, and utilities, if you did not scale up, others did, leaving laggards exposed to shrinking market shares and economies of scale too high to compete with the larger enterprises. Customers encouraged the process by demanding their suppliers provide services wherever they (customers) are. If you rent cars from Hertz, you want Hertz wherever you go in the world. Banking services within nations, such as the large market making up the United States, became the premier example of scaling up through M&As, using IT to make it all work.

While discussing how companies are scaling up through M&As, I should note that one can partner, or use technology, to accomplish the same task. Remember Amazon.com and books? After this firm got into the book business, it quickly realized that readers also bought CDs, and so the firm started to sell music to the same audience and, in the process,

ments in such diverse countries as Ireland and Malaysia. Economic progress in the 1990s vindicated the tinkering with the pre-World War II industrial capitalist model that was well underway and which matured during the period of the Cold War.

This tinkering resulted, for example, in extensive deregulation of many industries: utilities, transportation, telephone, telecommunications, trucking, utilities, even public education. All through the 1980s and 1990s, government agencies privatized, such as the U.S. Postal Service (USPS), one of the largest public privatizations in the world. Even the Chinese are doing it. However, the Russians hold the world record for recent privatization, with thousands of government-owned facilities now out of public ownership, done in their mad rush toward a capitalist economic structure.

Productivity of labor and capital increased all through the 1990s in the forms of downsizing and process reengineering. These trends occurred simultaneously by the realignment of business missions and objectives, and the implementation of mass customization and new forms of production (e.g., using the Toyota manufacturing model). These activities were at the heart of many quality management practices of the 1980s, lay-offs in the 1990s, and creation of as many new jobs increasingly more dependent on computer and other technology-based skills.

Further integration of global cash flows and the continued increase in capital availability around the world over the past 40 years also facilitated rapid exploitation of potentially profitable markets when combined with telecommunications. Opportunities are normally not constrained by national frontiers as in earlier decades. Free trade, cheap capital, relatively good transportation, and effective telecommunications networks have, instead, had the unintended consequence of making information-based skills and use of knowledge management strategies crucial success features for many businesses today.

In a series of studies conducted by IBM, beginning in the mid-1990s and nicknamed Watershed, the company's management consultants searched on an industry-by-industry basis

the quality gurus were right: Businesses are paying very close attention to the needs and wants of customers.

If the value net, then, is the organizational artifact of the networked age, what does it look like? Is this the construct managers are moving fast toward? The answers are only just beginning to emerge, and it is not clear that the picture we have is correctly described. But we know some things.

First, the new value chains are dynamic, fluid, and involve multiple enterprises. Michael Porter's original model of the 1970s and 1980s is sitting on top of a footprint encompassing many organizations and undergoes rapid transformation.

Second, in this emerging environment the best focus is on the core competencies of the business rather than on simply leveraging existing assets. That means firms create value in the market with more than a product or service. They rely more on their ability to coordinate cost effectively across a variety of cross-unit dependencies. These dependencies are suppliers, substitutors, customers, and complementors. Suppliers can be both internal and external. Substitutors are competitors and outsourcers. To senior executives today these are probably the most obvious element of the equation. Competitors in this new world are most familiar to line management and employees; they are the rivals who rapidly take away value add through the use of networks (e.g., remember the early rounds of competition between booksellers Amazon.com and Barnes and Noble?). Customers may be new, different, or continuous. Complementors are those who significantly influence who becomes a customer or supplier, such as advertisers, business partners, and other satisfied customers.

Emerging as the key to success is a firm's ability to be flexible and cost effective. A company must be both simultaneously. Direct access and accountability in the marketplace leads to a firm learning very quickly how it is doing, and to rapidly understand its value add. It is also becoming clear that the definition of value add changes, often frequently, hence creating a need for flexibility in responding to market conditions. Speeding up delivery of the right services and goods, and doing so cost effectively, becomes even more of an imperative

and best known new Internet brands of the 1990s, or Dell, one of the newest technology brands of the same decade. There is also the requirement to undermine those who would lock them out through advertising and capturing mind share. Because everything speeds up and has a shorter life cycle in this new period, case studies of success and failure are already numerous. For many, the story is one of eliminating physical assets and employees in exchange for electronic access and construction of value nets. The very earliest example, dating back a decade before the Internet, yet network-based, was the ATM terminal, which replaced the bricks and mortar of branch banks and tellers. Now, picture a similar phenomenon across many industries, but instead of with an ATM, a personal computer that costs less than $1,000. Get your customers to order their own airplane tickets off the Internet, for example, and you eliminate the need for some ticket agents; show homes over the Internet and you reduce the number of real estate agents needed. Bottom line: goodbye geography and manpower, hello Internet access.

GLOBALIZATION AND DIGITALIZATION

So IT expenditures are up all around the world. Castells, the NUA Internet surveys, and government forecasts in the USA and from OECD countries all report the same thing. The world is continuing its long-standing tradition of integrating economic activity, transportation, and communications.

Normally, discussions of globalization of business and the role of the computer chip—what I refer to as digitalization—are not seen together, but they are inextricably linked. The reason is relatively straightforward: To a large extent, deployment of computer chips in products, transportation, and the all-important collection of communications tools has really moved globalization from being either a loose affair, or rhetoric, to a hard, tangible reality. This situation is relatively new. To be sure, globally based trade has been going on for centuries. Camels loaded with spices from Asia were regularly led

Commentators on today's business environment have all discussed one or another of these aspects, but usually not together. All four are simultaneously influencing the nature of commerce and the hunt for new value propositions, with each influencing the other. All four are profoundly affected by digital tools, about which I have more to say later.

One very obvious trend has been the increased availability of many types of products, with far more options than fifty, twenty, or even ten years ago. For example, in the 1950s in the United States, there were five national brands of carbonated soft drinks: Coca-Cola, Pepsi-Cola, Orange Crush, Dr. Pepper, and 7-Up. (Root beer and ginger ale are not considered carbonated drinks.) How many dozens are available today? Now add in scores of variations of bottled teas, fruit juices, and water. Even for very new things that did not exist a generation ago, there is variety. For instance, a person can buy nearly 150 brands of personal computers, although a half dozen dominate the market. Television came into our homes forty years ago using antennas, then it became possible twenty years ago to use cable as well. Next we could add a satellite dish as yet a third option. Today cable is available from cable companies, utilities, and telephone providers. Dishes can be acquired from telephone companies, electrical utilities, and from retail outlets selling electronic products. Once dishes were big and cost over $10,000 each; now they are the size of a food platter and cost less than $300. While most observers of the new landscape rightfully point out that consumers today face wider choices (hence greater complexity in their hunt for values), so, too, do providers of goods and services.

To a large extent variety is driven by the capability of manufacturers and service providers to offer custom-made goods for the same price as mass-produced or common services. That is the basic idea behind mass customization, which began in the 1980s in manufacturing and now is embedded deeply in services as well. In manufacturing, use of technology (and, yes, the computer chip) made it possible to make customized products for individual customers at the same price as mass produced ones.[14] In may parts of the world, our expectations have reached a point where specific offerings rel-

customers it is the only unchanging rock they can cling to in their search for quality and a fair price.

Third, global visibility of products, services, and pricing offers customers the potential to build their own pricing and value propositions. Some personal computers are made to order, no two have to be intentionally alike in configuration or price. Blue jeans can be cut and sewn to fit a customer's body precisely; homes are designed online and then physically constructed. In each case, the use of modeling tools to design and price, and then the use of software to manufacture or deliver, are what make it cost effective (or priced right) to tailor.

Four, branding or co-branding and private labeling approaches are on the rise to target markets of one or few customers. This trend is a byproduct of individual customers defining their own needs and values, coupled with renewed branding initiatives by providers.

Fifth, questions are being raised about whether companies should differentiate products they make by adding services and knowledge to them. The response is increasingly yes, because of the global trend toward mass customization. Who today would offer to sell a car or major appliance without ranges of service support?

Now, let's deal with the decline of physical markets, which I think is a far more precise way to speak about global economics because it affects the work of managers. Historically, selling and buying took place somewhere, in a store, market, even on a street corner, but usually at a predetermined spot on earth. People made goods, moved these to a store, customers bought them, and hauled them home or to work. Increasingly, we are seeing the disembowelment of physical markets. In less prosaic language, what is happening is that the eye-to-eye, face-to-face contact between buyer and seller is either being replaced or supplemented by different approaches. The most obvious at the moment is electronic commerce. It is easy to exaggerate here, since Internet purchasing is expanding at the moment at a very rapid rate. To be sure, the vast majority of sales are done the old-fashioned way, with customers going to stores to make their purchases. But retailers are having to deal

important in influencing the buying decision. Price is important too, but freshness first. If sold remotely—as increasingly is happening in the USA during the Christmas holiday season—we eliminate the physical experience. So how do we establish freshness? Guarantees? Fabulous photographs? Reputation (branding)? Other questions concern packaging for delivery, support, and selling techniques in a virtual market. What is a customer conditioned by previous prices willing to pay for delivery in a virtual market? Will a customer pay five to ten percent more in exchange for convenience of delivery to home or office? They pay that much additional for fast delivery, but what about for convenience? Does the answer vary by type of product, time, or industry? Since discounting is already widely evident on the Internet, do they want the combined purchase and delivery costs to be below what they would have paid in a physical market? So far, what is clear is that they want lower prices and are getting them.

The point is, there is a growing set of new issues and implications for management to address. The decline of physical commerce suggests some obvious ones:

- Value chains for manufacturing, marketing, and delivery of goods and services change.

- Loss of the physical market. What are the *new value* propositions?

- Potential effects on brand loyalty and familiarity also change when goods and services are sold remotely. How do they change? Does that hurt or help the firm?

- Recourse for consumers wanting to replace a defective product. How do you do that? Who enforces quality standards, a government agency where the consumer is or where the vendor sells or makes the product? How is the market able to enforce standards via competition? The economists are not sure how to answer this last question.

- Role of government safety and taxing authority changes. Look at the current debate about what to do with sales taxation of Internet-based commerce underway in the

hence the notion of parallelism. Old markets stay or disappear at various rates over a long period of time. New ones do too, existing, however, parallel to older ones. The consequence is economic strains for all, and some confusion for those of us who must describe the market landscape, a messy process. There is the traditional vendor experiencing new forms of competition, a new supplier attempting to gain market share before traditional rivals can react or exit, and the customer facing so many new options yet fearful of not getting the "best deal."

However, the critical observation is that the move to electronic markets is a one-time phenomenon. Just like the move to books and away from manuscripts was a one-time process (one that took less than 50 years to accomplish), so too is the current generation of workers faced with conversion to the electronic in similar historic proportions. Once done, issues of the predigitized world will have been displaced by those related to electronics and not solely to paper-based, physically planted economics.

You can expect three phases in the process. The first, the one we were always in, is the predigital market. Then, the one we are entering now, which is a combination of physical markets and electronic markets (e.g., buying and selling on the Internet). The electronic markets have much of the same look and feel of the physical markets (e.g., prices, terms and conditions). Electronic-based text looks like paper-based documents too, with pages and paragraphs. But a third phase will begin when electronic formats dominate the physical and paper. That phase will begin by looking like things from the past, but then, as we learned from experience with the digital, new ways of expression, new formats for presenting information, different value propositions, and new terms and conditions will emerge. Those will remain a partial mystery for some time, however.

But back to my basic point of why the conversion to the electronic is fundamentally a one-time event for management over the next couple of decades. The case to move is a compelling one. Second, we have seen this kind of historic shift

- New competitors arriving with no investments in the past or in buildings and inventories. These include all the new Internet-based companies, such as eBay.

- New sources of rapid wealth and poverty. Examples are the developers of Netscape who became millionaires, and mini-computer manufacturers who began to go out of business.

- People picking and choosing what to use and when. Buying a car online at midnight, while using software to find the best financing, rapidly becoming widely evident examples.

- Transitions while running with more than one option, finding it expensive and complicated. This is the circumstance faced by retail operators who are selling goods through stores and on the Internet at the same time. They sell at retail prices in brick and mortar operations but are forced to sell the same goods online for as much as 40 percent less.

These various parallel implications and issues of the transition were evident in different forms in earlier times. As the transitions were completed, they were replaced with new issues and implications that reflected the new realities. Those new circumstances in turn opened up vast new areas of opportunities and innovations. The move to the printed page in the 1500s, for example, created the publishing industry while also leading to the creation of the printed book.

Managers are asking several questions. What cost-effective supply chains or channels of distribution should be used, and when? How many lines of business should they have? What remains profitable from existing lines of business? They worry about the roles of scale and scope both in regard to investment commitments and market reach. We know today that those investments are very different in form and size from those of even such a recent time as the start of the 1990s. These investments are also tied to the larger issue of what products to offer and to what extent they are customized. There is also the most obvious, underlying risk of all, the actual move to a new order.

computer chips became the backbone of many automated and semi-automated business processes in almost every medium to large corporation and government agency in the world, even in underdeveloped nations. Second, they made possible the installation of multifunction telephone networks (e.g., call waiting, call traffic analysis, and call traffic load balancing). Most important with telephone networks, computer chips made it possible to convert these networks from mere voice transmission systems into the complex networks of today that allow us to display text and pictures, not just numbers, and ultimately, the availability of the Internet. Third, chip capacity made it possible to enhance man–machine interaction, which means one can use computers to work with customers or suppliers in a growing range of applications, such as automated voice response systems which we now use when we ask for telephone directory assistance or leave phone messages.

Another set of issues relates to the degree to which this technology has been deployed. It is absolutely correct to say that it is ubiquitous throughout the industrialized world and rapidly becoming so in less developed countries, thanks to cell phones and small appliances. Look at any middle-class home in Western Europe or in the United States and you find computer chips in such appliances as the microwave oven, in digital clocks, stereo equipment, in the washer and dryer (especially in Europe), compact disk players, refrigerators, toasters, bread makers, coffeemakers, telephone answering machines, telephones, cameras, VCRs, and portable tape recorders. An increasingly evident consequence is our growing familiarity with intelligent machines helping people move through the activities of their daily lives. More and more individuals are coming to understand and to be comfortable with what computer chips are doing for them. For another, chips (integrated circuits) are making it possible for humans to dictate to equipment (and hence to vendors of such equipment) what activities they want these machines and services to perform. Our power also extends to the speeds at which we want these tasks performed.

How long can this go on? In theory, for a long time, because whatever replaces the chip will have to do more. But let's look

by professors, journalists, and social commentators. It is also the one subject most management and process teams think they understand best about this new network-centric economy. The key points are:

- Information about customers, products, and markets can be applied to make different products and create newer, better, more economically attractive services, often by shifting information to a customer so that he or she can do some of the work of selecting, self-selling, implementing, and using goods.
- For manufacturers, the ability to differentiate products by attaching information to them, or additional services, is a differentiator in an age when almost any competitor can build a reliable product at a competitive price.
- Applied information and knowledge can lead to incremental sources of income.
- Customers are demanding more information and training in use of products.

We see these elements at work all the time. Niche markets are more defined. Shipping a piece of software with built-in tutorials, finding incremental revenue through services, or offering recipes with food people buy are all early manifestations of the informationalization of products and services. A very early, paper-based example was the practice of soup manufacturers to print recipes for their products on the can's label (e.g., Campbell Soup in the United States).[20] In the next two chapters I explore the issue of computer chips in more places than ever by looking in greater detail at the role of best practices, knowledge workers, and the extent to which they produce value through insight, often underpinned by use of tools that have computer chips in them. But the important message to take away from this page is that many vendors are injecting information into or around their products and services, not simply into their internal processes and tasks. The role of information is becoming a major element in the construction of new value propositions.

some changes stimulated by technology. Some trends that are significant are both political and social. Parallelisms operate here too. Some nations are more democratic than others, societies vary in their approval of women in the workforce, some are more inclined toward open dissemination of information than their neighbors, and so forth. Even then, there are some emerging realities to contend with that have a global quality to them.

First, the world has generally moved into a period of representative government. This process began in the eighteenth century and has not yet fully played out. With the increase in various forms of democratic governments has come additional support for freedom of economic action for self-gain of the type evident in successful capitalist economies. In the past twenty years, all but one of Latin America's 21 governments have become representative in form.[21] The Soviet Union's authoritarian government gave way to one clearly attempting to be more democratic. The fact that its various states are in a period of confusion, difficult transition, and even civil war, should not mislead one into thinking that big chunks of the European parts of the old Soviet Union necessarily reject democracy and capitalism. The American colonies went through a similar period of chaos during the years of the Confederation (1780s), and they turned out to be a strong, powerful nation—a result that would have been difficult to anticipate in that turbulent decade. Even China is compelled to leave well enough alone in Hong Kong and to encourage capitalist economic behavior in its eastern provinces. For businesses, that means fewer barriers to the free flow of information and a further opening of economic opportunities. It is also not outside the bounds of reality that democratic forms of government may give way to other regimes, as there are no guarantees.

But there will continue to be problems. Juan J. Linz and Alfred Stepan, two very distinguished political scientists who have done some of the most comprehensive analysis of the nature of both totalitarian and democratic regimes, have warned that a range of governmental structures will remain for a long period of time. While they are obvious in their acknowl-

remain a critical requirement. Opportunities will come online in new places over an extended period of time. The dream of selling every Chinese citizen a cell phone and a PC is just wishful thinking. However, selling Digital Economy products and services to several million Chinese members of the emerging middle class in East Asia is not.

Third, the number of potential customers is rising, although in what today we would argue are the poorest sections of the world. The wealthiest sectors are experiencing demographic stabilization, as populations reach zero or low growth, such as in North America and in Western Europe. The poorest, on the other hand, such as in Africa and Latin America, are surging with growth. India and China have implemented population control programs that are finally showing results. In the case of China, that trend will increase the average family's standard of living over the next quarter century. The same may happen to a lesser degree in parts of the Indian subcontinent, barring an unforeseen disaster, such as nuclear war or some medical catastrophe.[25] The implication is clear here too: Markets will appear within countries on the one hand, while on the other, products and services will have to decline in offering price for their demand to increase. Both represent opportunities and challenges to any firm attempting to participate in the global market.

So much for the big picture. What about values and social changes? I assume that most readers of this book are either American or Western European. The Americans understand their culture and how it functions in a free economy because it has been relatively stable, with no civil wars, massive internal migrations, or foreign invasions for a long time. However, OECD studies, among others, suggest Western and Central Europeans may not understand how much they have changed since World War II. A quick look at some of those changes suggest what they look like as they move toward a more unified Europe with a market of over 350 million customers in the immediate future, and possibly as many as 400 million if nations on the fringe of Europe participate. On many levels Western Europeans represent the model for the sorts of social changes underway in Central and Eastern Europe, to a lesser

Between 1970 and 1990, women's civil liberties expanded. Women acquired the right to use birth control means, to own property, and to divorce in every Catholic country in Western Europe—all within one generation. The requirement that children stay in school increased by, on average, more than one additional year into their late teens. Every government made massive investments in education at all levels. Western Europe experienced the largest growth in university student populations in its history. In some universities, women dominated the student population. Social attitudes changed toward divorce, childrearing, careers, religion, education, and politics. At the risk of gross generalization, the move was liberal, modern, urban, urbane, and closer to what Americans, for example, look like in their large urban centers.[27]

What do these enormous changes mean to businesses? The most fundamental implication is that nearly 75 million new consumers were created—people who have jobs, buy automobiles, refrigerators, manufactured clothing, watch televisions that they own, use cell phones, go out to dinner, buy groceries in stores, and are increasingly educated, urbane, and socially mobile. In short, a large group of new customers entered the market. That development occurred in a half century of enormous prosperity for Europe, a time in which many countries experienced annual economic growth of over four percent. The historically profound movement underway to create a unified Europe will play out first in the marketplace, not in politics (although it is the political that seems to get all the attention), creating a market even larger than the one that exists in North America. Anytime tens of millions of affluent customers can be added to potential markets, that is news. That is what has happened in Europe. Already the Internet is forcing unification as customers from across Europe buy goods online from vendors in many countries, soon paying for these with the Euro and using their Visa or Mastercard credit cards! This development has spawned all kinds of pseudo-official and governmental inquiries, from that of the German government to the European Union and OECD, to determine what public policies should be implemented. In short, the politicians are

change in human activity as any we have seen in the past 500 years; it makes everybody's short list.

Managers and employees of any enterprise at all levels from a clerk to a brand-new MBA to a seasoned CEO are, thus, being handed the opportunity to think of vast portions of the earth as their markets, an access that is as realistic and at least as convenient to reach as the ones they had before. In fact, and increasingly, firms are already doing just that—thinking globally—leading to new levels of scale and scope that will force some companies out of business because their markets remained just national. It will be a process similar to the one which occurred, for example, when national markets were created in the United States in the late nineteenth and early twentieth centuries, driving many regional companies out of business or to be absorbed by firms operating on a national scale. So what we have learned about scale and scope once again will have to be applied quickly over the next decade or more as effective participation moves from the national to the international. Problems of language, law, and local custom will have to be resolved. Mass customization techniques will help, so will some of the new business practices that are emerging. The Swiss company ABB's requirement that all its managers work in the English language is a harbinger of things coming as corporations strive to come up with global practices and policies, suggesting that there may be a further homogenization of business practices around the world. These will also have to work within the context of local cultures. Not everybody is an American or a Western European!

Technology will be the glue that holds many things together. Internationally imposed accounting practices, reporting business results via satellites, and using the Internet to communicate, perform, sell, and service are increasingly a new way of life. Companies will have to learn how to form economic alliances in multiple cultures and nations while identifying hot spots of economic opportunity, such as in East Asia (not all of China), portions of the old Soviet Union (not all 17 former republics), portions of South Africa (but not all of sub-Sahara Africa), and so forth. This change is more than Ford Motor or IBM designing products in one or more countries and building

ENDNOTES

1. For example, Peter F. Drucker, *Managing in Turbulent Times* (New York: Harper & Row, 1980), Charles Handy, *The Age of Unreason* (Boston: Harvard Business School Press, 1989).

2. Often, the success of America was framed in the language of technological supremacy, with science the handmaiden of the practical. See, for example, Carrol Pursell, *The Machine in America: A Social History of Technology* (Baltimore: Johns Hopkins University Press, 1993).

3. Jonathan Hughes, *American Economic History* (Glenview, Ill.: Scott, Foresman and Company, 1997): 502–503, 517–525.

4. William J. Baumol, Sue Anne Batey Blackman, and Edward N. Wolff, *Productivity and American Leadership: The Long View* (Cambridge, MA: MIT Press, 1989): 143–159; see also James W. Cortada, *Info-America* (forthcoming).

5. A team of scholars has recently documented America's road to the Information Age, beginning with the 1700s, in Alfred D. Chandler, Jr. and James W. Cortada (eds.), *A Nation Transformed by Information: How Information Has Shaped the United States from Colonial Times to the Present* (New York: Oxford University Press, 2000).

6. A possible exception is music, which was noisy, but which also came into our lives in greater quantity thanks to such technological innovations as digital instruments and the Internet.

7. The U.S. Bureau of Labor Statistics did begin at the end of the 1990s to define this new economy, starting by describing classes of work and followed with measures of productivity.

8. Alan Stone, *How America Got On-Line: Politics, Markets, and the Revolution in Telecommunications* (Armonk, NY: M.E. Sharpe, 1997): 114–115; U.S. Department of Commerce, *The Emerging Digital Economy II* (Washington, D.C.: U.S. Government Printing Office, June 1999).

9. I have explored this in considerable detail in "Info-America: The Use of Information in Modern America" (forthcoming).

10. Leslie Kaufman, "Amazon to Remake Itself Into a Bazaar on the Internet," *The New York Times*, September 30, 1999, Internet edition, http://nytimes.com.

21. As of this writing (2000), the one holdout is Fidel Castro's Cuba.

22. Juan J. Linz and Alfred Stephan, *Problems of Democratic Transition and Consolidation* (Baltimore: Johns Hopkins University Press, 1996), first quote p. 435, second quote p. 457.

23. Ibid.

24. Based on World Bank data reproduced in Kenichi Ohmae, *The End of the National State: The Rise of Regional Economies* (New York: Free Press, 1995): 90–92.

25. Demographic considerations are often ignored by senior executives as they plan the futures of their firms. For an introduction to current trends and implications, see W.W. Rostow, *The Great Population Spike and After: Reflections on the 21st Century* (New York: Oxford University Press, 1998).

26. Paul Bairoch, *Economics and World History: Myths and Paradoxes* (Chicago: University of Chicago Press, 1993): 126–132, 167–168. The distinguished political scientist Samuel P. Huntington has recently begun to emphasize our need to understand the role of culture in global politics and economics. See, for example, his most recent book, *The Clash of Civilizations and the Remaking of World Order* (New York: Simon & Schuster, 1996).

27. These case studies are explained in detail in James N. Cortada and James W. Cortada, *Can Democracy Survive in Western Europe?* (Westport, Conn: Greenwood Press, 1996).

28. His books include *Strategy and Structure* (Cambridge, Mass.: MIT Press, 1962); *The Visible Hand: The Managerial Revolution in American Business* (Cambridge, Mass.: Harvard University Press, 1977); *Scale and Scope: The Dynamics of Industrial Capitalism* (Cambridge, Mass.: Harvard University Press, 1990).

WAVES OF LEARNING, WAVES OF BEST PRACTICES

The essence of knowledge is, having it, to apply it; not having it, to confess your ignorance.

CONFUCIUS

 Expanded overt reliance on knowledge and skills believed to enhance competitive advantages represents one of the most important transformations in the operations of corporations during the past half century. There has also been an enormous increase in the availability and use of data (information), but this trend should not be confused with knowledge, which is the insight and understanding that comes from having data, experience, and organized ways of analyzing information. As organizations became larger and more complex in structure, managers acquired vast quantities of information about their firms, industries, and markets. The accumulation of large quantities of potentially valuable information was particularly the case with *Fortune* 1000 firms, many of which have thousands of employees, have been in business for years, and operate in many countries.

By the end of the twentieth century, corporate competencies had become not only a subfield of business knowledge, but also a body of practices that showed managers and their employees how to become more insightful about their work. Today, understanding and exploiting corporate competencies is considered an essential element of sound business practices, recognized as such by all levels of management across all industries. The debate is over; it is an excellent thing to be good at. How that acceptance of the value of corporate competencies came about and its relevance to an information-rich economy is crucial to any understanding of how companies can compete in the future. Closely related to this insight is one brought over from economic and historical studies that suggests changes in industries and economies often come in waves. These waves vary in size and length, but nonetheless point to patterns of behavior that can stimulate action. In short, it is part of what people speak of today when they think about the notion of knowledge management.

While much of what I said in the last two paragraphs may sound obvious, less so is the fact that the volume of information an individual has to review and apply is growing. The rate at which best practices are developed, then changed, is also increasing. If you told an engineer in 1948 that what was learned as a student would be significantly outdated in less than a decade by the 1980s, you would not have been believed. But that is what happens today. Medical practice and knowledge double every four to five years. What many do not realize is that when new medical knowledge and practices emerge, prior medical knowledge is obsolete. Old knowledge and practices increasingly are competitive disadvantages as firms move from the Second Industrial Age into portions of the new Information Age. Thus, it is rate, speed, and currency of knowledge and best practices that are the central topics of concern to management today when they talk about learning organizations.

Lashing competencies and knowledge together has increasingly been accomplished by using the tools of process management. Particularly in very large enterprises, but also in many mid-sized firms around the world, application of process

them to succeed. The lessons vary by industry. For example, in pharmaceuticals the complex body of knowledge about how to develop and bring new drugs to market made it possible for established firms to preserve their original new entrant (dominant) advantages over the course of nearly one century. On the other hand, both in the consumer electronics industry and in the personal computer business, where entrants come and go, surviving and failing is based on a different set of learnings. American firms developed many of the technologies and products of the consumer electronics industry, such as RCA with television. The Japanese learned those technologies, how to build and market these products, and ultimately dominated the consumer electronics industry. Today, that industry has almost no U.S. base; it is overwhelmingly dominated by the Japanese. Today a similar battle is underway in the pharmaceutical industry between firms in the United States and Western Europe; the outcome is yet uncertain. The battle will not be won or lost based on who has more capital to invest. The war will be decided by the combination of capabilities (knowledge) and prowess applied to the control of the market. Knowing the lessons of success within one's industry, and building on these, are crucial for the long-term success of any firm or manager. These are new insights for today's companies.[2] But let us begin with a basic building block of knowledge that every new employee coming into a firm today faces: corporate competencies.

RISE OF THE COMPETENCY-BASED ENTERPRISE

Why should you care about the history of competency-based enterprises? Why not just summarize the findings of some business professor who has studied the issue? Isn't it enough to understand what they are and how they work? These are fair questions, and they have much merit. Business school professors have studied this topic extensively, particularly during the 1980s and 1990s, and consultants working

tent as a manufacturer, or is it also competent in metallurgy? Although it started out as a mining company, eventually senior management of 3M decided the firm knew a great deal about the chemistry of adhesives. The realization that organizations have collective competencies came in the years just before World War II, surfaced in business literature by the early 1960s, and then served as the subject of much managerial theory and practice in the 1970s and 1980s. By the 1980s we also began to see a growing body of publications on strategy for competing on competencies. Since then we have all experienced an enormous flowering of interest in the subject.[3] However, I can also safely observe that this body of understanding is relatively new and, thus, holds the potential of expanding as experience and additional studies point out other management tasks and best practices.

With the realization that organizations had competencies, managers and academics began codifying them. For Western industrialized firms, professors began to define the subtle capabilities of a business organization. For instance, Theodore Levitt, one of the most influential business professors of our century, asked what role firms played and what they did well: Were you a car manufacturer or in transportation? Mission statements came into their own within two decades of these kinds of questions being asked as a byproduct of managers working on organizing enterprises around focused objectives. Along the way, managers discovered that their firms had less obvious competencies that held the potential of economic value. For example, for decades most managers inside and outside of IBM thought that the core competence of that firm was the manufacture and sale of large computers. Today, the more astute would argue—and be supported by historians who have looked at IBM—that one of the great competencies of the company is packaging technology into highly manufacturable forms. Once management recognized this competency, it became easier to consider creating an OEM business, something it did in the 1990s, generating billions of dollars in incremental revenue. McDonald's, the fast food restaurant chain, has a core competence in cooking hamburgers and french fries. But, upon closer examination, one could argue that

Benchmarking also identified ways in which a firm could do something less expensively than a potential rival, who could be implementing a different business model where their operating costs were already below those of the firm offering to do the same work. In the end, managers had to be very selective in what they offered to do: IBM running large data centers, AT&T running telephone networks, ADP handling payroll, credit card companies handling billing, utilities managing large numbers of service accounts. In hindsight, to be successful in the outsourcing business, a firm had to:

- Have been doing something very well for a while
- Be perceived by others as especially competent in the process being offered
- Be seen as continuing to retain and enhance this offering as the company's own core competency
- Have the capability to sell and service the core competency
- Provide it for less cost than most other outsourcing competitors

In the end, merchandising a company's competencies is still a wonderful business opportunity, a way to offset fixed costs of providing services to the rest of your firm.

Another strategy emerged, involving the acquisition of competencies complementing what already exists in an enterprise. That strategy has had mixed results too, but is very popular. One reflection of its application is outsourcing. For instance, if your IT organization and applications are relatively stable, and you are not a technology firm, you probably would look at IBM, AT&T, EDS, or to others to take over operation of your data centers and networks. Or, as an alternative, if you absolutely need to be outstanding in some process or delivery of a product or service, you might form an alliance, partnership, or acquire a firm already possessing the competency. Microsoft, for example, acquired over a dozen firms that have information databases and other information assets (e.g., photographs) that it could use. Dismantling or selling off divisions and businesses often is triggered by the perception that the unit to be discarded had competencies incompatible with

ready for you to jump into and drive off without filling out forms or standing in line. In fact, this is a standard level of performance by Hertz. As a traveler, you quickly realize that there is no reason to stand in line for travel-related services; Hertz proved that.

This experience can have negative consequences for other firms, hotels for instance. They do not see Hertz as a rival, just a complementary firm that is part of a much larger web of businesses that support travelers. Now, as that traveler, get back in a long line to check in or out of a hotel on that same trip when you rented a car from Hertz, and you can imagine how you feel about the hotel's service. The hotel management, since many insufficiently understand their customers, particularly frequent travelers, may not realize that while standing in line to check in is very common across the hotel industry, that Hertz just created a new level of expectation on the part of the hotel's customer. As that same traveler you know you do not like to stand in line at a bank, grocery store, airline, or to get into a restaurant. You know there is a better way. The lesson: Firms need to know the less obvious sources of competition or influences on customer expectations, in this case Hertz. But Hertz is in the rental car business, not the hotel business or airline industry.

Computers provide another illustration of the complexities involved. Because IBM is a leading manufacturer of computers,[4] you would say it experiences competition from Hewlett-Packard (H-P), Dell, Compaq, Hitachi, and so forth, all manufacturers of various types and sizes of computers. This observation would be correct, but only absolutely true through the mid-1990s, after which the firm had changed so much, along with its mix of products, that other observations about competition would have to be added. All these computers use chips, are manufactured in roughly the same way, and, at the time, were sold in well-understood ways. This is a competency-based view of the computer industry and its members. But if you looked at other industries, you would find similar capabilities applied differently, suggesting potential avenues of new competitive strengths. For example, every leading manufacturer of automobiles has many of the same technical skills as

Relevant competencies can be found across many industries, so no one can afford to look just within his or her own industry for insight. People did not arrive at these two lessons overnight; they had been emerging over the course of the past half century. As you will see later with knowledge management, the environment necessary to reach such observations has been emerging over the course of nearly a century.

Another conclusion, therefore, is that an increased awareness of historical trends within a firm, traditional industry, and in neighboring parts of an economy (both firms and markets) becomes a crucial body of knowledge that managers and their employees need to leverage regularly if they are to thrive in the era we are entering. As has long been the case, those who can use historical perspective often enjoy many advantages, even first entrants. This truth applies both to services and to manufacturing. The need for historical perspective on one's own competencies and those of rivals is more essential in services businesses because patterns of skills are less understood there than in manufacturing. Institutional memories are often quite short due to the relatively high turnover in personnel typical in this sector of the economy. A second reason is related to the fact that as managers and students of business, we have had more experience with manufacturing than with service sector corporations. The service sector of the world's economy came into its own as a dominant or nearly dominant feature in some nations only since World War II. Thus, as we are just learning how to understand and exploit enterprise-wide competencies, we also have to understand simultaneously the nature of service sector firms.

Looking across the fence at someone else's industry does reveal some effective practices. For example, the pharmaceutical industry teaches how to retain first entrant advantages for decades. The computer hardware business offers models of how to sell and support complex products. Consumer electronics teaches us about product innovation and branding. Utilities, banking, and transportation are industries in which one can learn mistakes, lessons, and innovative ways to move from regulated to deregulated markets. Banking, particularly in the United States, and publishing in Europe, are hotbeds of

that industry. But if you are going to rely increasingly on knowledge management practices, it is imperative to understand how these are transforming commerce. The fact is, these practices are creating many changes that help spur a firm into the vortex of the Information Age.

HOW KNOWLEDGE MANAGEMENT IS TRANSFORMING COMMERCE

In the world of business, knowledge is about insight based on the combination of experience, context, and data. It is the understanding people have about the world they occupy. For an organization, knowledge management is about organizing the use of what is in an employee's mind in some coordinated fashion for the betterment of the firm. For both individuals and firms, relevance of knowledge is gauged by its applicability to the creation of value and wealth. Jack Welch, CEO at GE, often admonished his managers to translate learnings into rapid action, believing that act of translation provides what he called "the ultimate competitive business advantage." Thomas H. Davenport and Laurence Prusak, two leading experts on knowledge management, view knowledge as a corporate asset, requiring managers to invest and protect it much like anything else of value, such as money, stocks, factories, and inventory. As new value propositions emerge over the next few years, sorting out the role of technological collections of systems such as the Internet (which facilitated many types of globalized business transactions and learnings) and informationalized products (such as computer-controlled machines), places an increasing premium on knowledge. Use of knowledge is already a differentiator for a corporation because so many firms can make good products or deliver fine service. However, being able to do new things quickly, and very well, become the differentiators. These require a group of knowledgeable employees organized in a way to get that done.[5]

There is also the question of efficiency. By using computer networks and imaging, for example, an increasing number of

underway; much remains to be done to define new management practices.

Managerial tasks which require exploiting knowledge can't wait. There are already actions that need to be taken to exploit opportunities in the new economy different from what existed in the Industrial Age. First, managers are beginning to recognize the strategic value of knowledge and are agreeing to protect and exploit it. This is more than traditional patent protections, this involves protecting and nurturing knowledge about their firms' core competencies. Second, employees at all levels of the enterprise are generating, codifying, and coordinating its accumulation, sharing this collection with those who need it the most to do their work. Third, traditional definitions of roles and skills—applied for decades—are taking on a knowledge twist. Fourth, and often done nearly first, executives are creating a digital infrastructure to support the movement of data around the organization. In turn, access to information is making employees more knowledgeable about what they must do and how.

What works well in this new world? For one thing, the practical manager begins with high-value knowledge, that is to say, collecting, preserving, and using information and insight which today most leverages capabilities of the organization in a competitive way. For another, like all good new initiatives, the best of these managers start slowly with highly defined projects—pilot programs and experiments—which they extend as people learn what works and why. For instance, the oil rig experts meet electronically several times to learn how best to attack complex engineering problems and then expand their meetings to deal with a wider variety of issues on a routine basis. Meanwhile, the insight from the original pilot project has generated information and observations that are transferred to other groups of engineers designing new oil rig platforms. Because speed in innovation is so crucial today, tinkering and experimenting along several fronts usually makes sense. The best managers and technical experts (e.g., engineers and consultants) install technological tools to facilitate collection and transfer of information. They create organizations that value and use knowledge (e.g., training programs,

ment the skills and speed with which an employee works, and to point out patterns and correlations. But ultimately, knowledge resides in the minds of people where implicit and explicit insights and information mix with tacit knowledge and experience, often in ways students of the human mind do not yet understand. Personnel practices and corporate cultures should deal with the acquisition and use of knowledge resident in brains. Corporate competencies are the organization's collective skills that transcend any individual. Managing these effectively calls for different business activities. The most crucial concern the tasks required to bring people together in groups such that, for example, it makes it possible for a competency to be used, or a collection of workers to design or build a product. For instance, bringing together all the experts on oil rig maintenance into some virtual community where they can learn from each other and mentor new employees doing the same kind of work is essential. Nurturing a corporate culture that facilitates levering competencies of the organization is equally important. For instance, if the firm knows how to sell globally, it must create measures and rewards that encourage global marketing and selling.

On the other hand, corporate competencies and knowledge management are different. Perhaps their most significant disparity concerns their rate of change. Corporate competencies change far more slowly than individual knowledge. Databases take time to reflect new entries, corporate beliefs about itself are often generational in duration, sometimes lasting a century or more.[10]

Personal knowledge does change and ultimately shrink in value. Remember the rate of new knowledge of doctors and the half-life of engineering knowledge? But the problem extends further than that. Professor Edward Wakin, of Fordham University, makes the point that knowledge is plastic. This is knowledge that can be used as plastic is used, not in a pejorative way, but as a thoroughly authentic contemporary body of insight useful right now. Like plastic, it can be molded under the heat of changing market realities, whenever a person can make knowledge work in different shapes and forms. Flexibility and utility make it plastic. It is a wonderful

wise efficient. What particularly lures management are metrics comparing performance of one organization to another. To a large extent, the concept of best practices, while a noble one because it inspires emulating the best, has frequently been over-hyped and poorly used as a business tool. Common sins include:

- Copying someone else's process exactly without taking into account that each organization's requirements are not exactly the same
- Adopting a practice because it is fashionable (e.g., employee suggestion systems, without thinking through how they should work in one's own organization
- Failing to link its performance to the needs of the enterprise
- Treating this as a one-time event

Often, people measure how their process works against some other organization's (benchmarking) and call that best practices. However, those who have gone through two or more decades of applying quality management have learned that best practices is a strategy, an ongoing, changing process of learning how others do things, then applying those findings where it makes sense in one's own department or firm. The key notion is strategy, followed by process. The metaphor of plastic applies here too because things change, as does what makes up a best practice as an organization or process evolves, learns, and improves.

For example, if you are trying to learn how to market using the Internet as a channel of distribution, then the issue is not about adopting Amazon.com's approach but rather learning from that firm what went well and what did not. Next, determine what makes sense from those findings applied to your firm. Finally, going back to learn about how people are using the Internet, not just simply comparing costs of transactions, leads to possible new and rapid deployment of changes. The process of learning continues in a never-ending iterative fashion. Searching for good ideas from others can be managed as a process itself, and the best managers routinely do this. As we transform from the business practices of the past half-century to new ones—often ones not completely clear to us—it

steps and jobs. Productivity rose measurably in many firms. It was good for its time, providing a rationale for downsizing when it needed to be done, improving efficiencies, and forcing a more intense appreciation of the performance of an organization. Currently, managements' concerns are more evident in building processes that allow them to do three things:

- Grow their business (revenue, profit, market share)
- Change offerings to meet shifting market realities
- Inject knowledge management into processes

All three actually reverse a trend of the early 1990s—reduction of work steps—by adding new ones in some instances, such as tasks to help with knowledge management.[13] So process design and change are very much a part of today's business mantra.

Managers and their employees increasingly see organizations as collections of processes. So the question has to be asked: Does one manage an enterprise or department differently in this new environment? The answer is both no and yes. No, in that much of what Peter Drucker taught us a generation ago about basic management responsibilities does not change. Roles and obligations remain the same. A manager is still responsible for setting direction and purpose, marshalling resources to implement those, and controlling the efficiency and effectiveness of such activities. Yes, in that process-centric companies are different than the most traditional hierarchical command-and-control world in which many of us grew up.

Four features characterize a process-centric company. First, many observers of managerial behavior see a profound shift in decision making from upper layers of managers downward toward those points in the enterprise closest to where decisions are implemented. Points in this context are either departments responsible for activities (e.g., creating and mailing bills) or groups of employees on the line who perform the actual work (e.g., warehouse and inventory control nonmanagement personnel). In other words, teams or individual employees are being granted authority and are being held more accountable for the results of tasks they perform,

widespread group decision making. Communal input, market studies, advice from consultants, and ultimately buy-in of the organization for a strategy have informed CEOs, but at the end of the day someone has to pick which mountain to climb and persuade the employees to scramble to its top. This situation had overwhelmingly been the case since the introduction of scientific management principles in the early decades of the twentieth century because this division of duties between senior and line management works.

The consequences and sound practices of the sea changes resulting from process management's role are significant. We are just now beginning to understand these. For example, if a team is held accountable for improving the performance of a process, that group of employees needs to own the data they collect on how their process is working so they can modify tasks as needed. If management retains ownership of data, it inadvertently motivates employees to hide bad news rather than put it on the table to be addressed by the process teams. Another point: Very quickly members of a team come to know more about a process and the economic ecology in which it operates than a manager who sits above that activity. As we move toward a work environment in which knowledge and skills are the coins of the realm, relative organizational political power and knowledge shifts from management to employees. Many managers do not understand that fundamental truth. Instead, they lead by telling, authorizing, and judging performance with less knowledge than their employees. Often the worst of these offenders are not open to new ideas. Their management style—telling, authorizing, and judging—is executed with less knowledge about a situation than what an employee has. We are learning that this style of management is bad practice in a process-centric organization. Processes fail, employees quit, and managers are fired.

Second, process management injects into daily activities such concepts as values and strategies of the organization. This is done by establishing well-articulated visions and objectives for a process and implementing measurement systems that track performance across a broad range of issues, using tools such as balanced score cards and statistical process con-

born out of the experience now of several decades of hard work by many corporations. Reality is propensity, not absolute alignment. Propensity can be measured through process management tools now in wide use, which place more emphasis on continuous improvement (read, alignment with management goals) and less on major blips in performance (both positive and negative) caused by such actions as process reengineering or outsourcing.

Third, processes become the nucleus of new organizational constructs. Traditional departments and divisions, always built to account for functions (e.g., sales and manufacturing) or around products and services (e.g., trucks vs. cars, consumer banking vs. commercial banking), change. Tension exists in the transformation because no established organization willingly melts away to be replaced by departments that in effect are made up of all the members of a process team. The Roman Empire, once in the process of full decay, still took 500 years to disappear, yet much changed in the way it functioned.[16]

Contemporary wisdom holds that the new Digital Economy causes businesses to come and go at warp speed. Yet the facts contradict this observation. There are some notable exceptions, of course, of companies that disappeared either because they were undercapitalized or were poorly managed. But even these firms died slowly. Once a powerhouse in the home appliance industry, Westinghouse took decades to vanish. RCA died slowly and painfully. Some firms nearly die and come back repeatedly: Apple Computer and TWA are two examples from the 1990s. The fact is many organizations still linger very long, protected by the logic that says a process often transcends any one organization, hence the need for more familiar structures. Most corporations that were successful in the Industrial Age are continuing to thrive in the emerging Information Age because they are well capitalized, properly run, and are innovating to take advantage of new technologies and business opportunities.

Firms stay in business longer for other reasons too. Bankruptcy laws in Western Europe and North America keep enter-

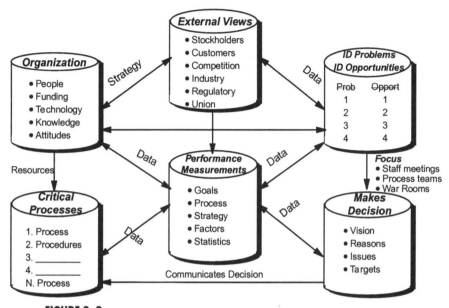

FIGURE 2–2
Organizational Supply Cabinet

tion and effective communications. The fact that ambiguity exists is more of a problem for senior executives than for line management or employees in general, but all three groups share nervousness about the transformation everyone is experiencing. Cultures of sharing (information and resources) are crucial, and their creation an essential activity for managers and executives. Without sharing, knowledge management, best practices, process improvements, alignment to objectives, voice of the customer, and speed in response to new market realities and opportunities, normally do not occur in either a timely or effective manner. Look at the companies that have disappeared since the early 1980s and you see the failure of sharing as one of the causes of their corporate demise. Communications, more than electronic mail or management messages, use a variety of vehicles that facilitate both sharing and exploitation of knowledge.[17]

Building into a company these four consequences (but also trends) calls for managers and workers in general to answer

they still pound on the shores of the beach. The analogy holds that economic behavior, such as inflation, while it never looks quite the same each time it occurs, has common features which, once you understand what they are, allow you to see when the next wave is coming. The theory holds that, like the child at the beach, you can then time the next good ride on a wave. A theme woven throughout this book is the frequently shifting nature of business environments. Understanding how to exploit change as opportunity is crucial to business success. That is why wave theories are important to understand and to leverage. It is also a body of knowledge virtually alien in the lexicon of management practices so far.

The concept is one useful to scientists as well who look for patterns of behavior leading to predictions about future activities in such things as weather, actions of living organisms, or the functioning of a physical phenomenon. The fact that waves of change are applied with positive results in the social sciences, economics, and history suggests it might help companies determine future patterns of work and opportunity. As of this writing (2000), I see almost no evidence of the model applied overtly in business. The one very clear exception is the methods of prediction now applied in gauging performance of processes using statistical process control. Given the way a process is designed and operates, it is very possible to predict within defined control limits how it will work tomorrow, next month, or even next year, so long as no element in the process is changed. This kind of prediction is well understood, and a strong body of best practices for it exists.[18]

Managers who have worked in business settings for more than two decades frequently think they see recurring patterns in business, typically cycles of good and bad times, inflation and even deflation, organizational changes that favor centralized vs. decentralized command-and-control, and so forth. To a certain extent they are right, because like the waves at a beach, no two cycles of business are quite the same but nonetheless are very familiar. One thing we all see quite frequently in business concerns sales: Do we deploy a direct sales force aligned by product, geography, or industry? Many twenty-plus-year sales veterans recall that they have witnessed all

changes before a less data-intensive industry, such as distribution. On the other hand, as the retail industry becomes increasingly dependent on data for marketing programs, it can learn from banks and insurance firms how to collect, manage, analyze, and protect data. High-tech firms like IBM can then teach them how to perform data mining, which is a fancy way of saying how to glean insights from that mountain of digitally stored information all these companies already collect. As historians study some of these data-intensive industries, such as is going on now with the insurance industry, we have the opportunity to identify waves of change useful in other industries.[19]

As change accelerates, time intervals between waves shorten. So we do not have to look at, for instance, price inflation of the seventeenth century caused by the influx of Spanish gold into Europe from the New World to understand what American inflation looked like in the 1970s during the presidency of Jimmy Carter. We have examples in our century of various levels of intensity to draw upon, such as the severe German inflation of the 1920s, the stubborn Brazilian inflation of the 1980s, and the effects of the swift monetary crisis in East Asia in 1998. The key is to understand patterns which, by definition, are collections of activities that occur over and over again. The notion of waves helps define why they never repeat exactly the same.[20]

David Hackett Fischer, a distinguished historian, spent many years cataloging economic characteristics of price waves, suggesting specific features we might want to think about as we explore how business waves affect our firms. These features concern duration, magnitude, and range. Several appear quite relevant.

- Change occurs in the rates of change, with prices, for instance, caused by expanding markets and institutionalized price increases.
- Ranges of annual fluctuations often diminish from one wave to another, such as the price ranges in highly available items (e.g., food in good times).

and firm, and whether they teach you something about how to run either your enterprise or a portion of it.

Fourth, become a student of the history and evolution of things relevant to your business. The most obvious candidate is telecommunications and the Internet, which means you should probably understand how the telegraph and telephone diffused throughout an economy and what the intended and unintended consequences were on firms, customers, and society in general. There is much economic and historical literature to inform the curious, and increasingly, information from business professors looking at case studies of the effects of specific technologies on business practices.[22] The richness of this kind of material and its easy accessibility is a relatively new phenomenon of the past two decades. These almost match in volume and value what has long been available to politicians and military officers.[23]

Fifth, exploit the notion of the prepared mind. Unfortunately this cannot be taught easily, but it can be encouraged as both an attitude and as a behavior, one that can be acquired over time. If you read widely across many subjects, not just about business, discuss business issues with others across numerous industries, and develop a knack for making sense of disparate pieces of information, patterns emerge which experience teaches you to act upon. The Warren Buffett type of manager is a good example of the individual who can take action based on this skill set. However, even if you do not believe you have the talent, others do have it and you can go to them for help. The key is to entertain diverse opinions from within and outside the enterprise about what is happening and determine how best to apply those observations in guiding business activity. To a large extent, this book is an exercise in this fifth step because it taps into economics, business practices, history and political science, quality management practices, information technology, and business experiences to create a description of business practices for the emerging business ecology.

Are there limits to historical insight and what we are learning about waves? There are several that cannot be denied. One of the limitations frustrating to managers is the fact that

IMPLICATIONS AND ACTIONS

The implications of this chapter reach to the heart of what concerns all practitioners of management: what stays the same, what changes. To state the obvious, the duties and responsibilities of management do not change. In fact, there is absolutely no evidence to suggest that the mission of management is fundamentally evolving. However, how duties are performed, and under what circumstances, are undergoing as much change as the profession of management has ever experienced. The change is also intensified by the fact that the activities of management are increasingly those of all workers, regardless of title or role. It is to the work of management that we must turn our attention.

First, today's managers and workers must learn the nuts and bolts of operating in a learning organization and how to manage through processes. Both activities now have wrapped around them a growing body of reliable practices, insights, and definable expectations that cut across most industries. To be sure, we all have much yet to learn. More business school professors and management consultants are at work on these topics today than in the history of the world. The growth in the number of experts on business who are conducting research using scientific principles is stunning. With thousands of contributors to the body of knowledge we are accumulating on business practices, we are finally reaching a point where we can begin to tentatively say management is more than art, although it has a great deal of the intuitive still about it. Expect to learn a great deal more about learning organizations in the future and to acquire an extensive body of factual material about best practices across the whole spectrum of process management and knowledge management.

A second implication for most workers at all stages of their careers is increasingly the requirement to take an intellectual, even an academic, view of their business. Because there is a body of knowledge about management and business practices, people have more to know and to study than ever before. This requires them to become students of their profession, reading

the Age of Information. Managers and their colleagues cannot be just smart or experienced. They have to know more and run enterprises that value the acquisition and rapid exploitation of insight.

It is no accident that Jack Welch sees applied knowledge as a strategic advantage. He is interested in ways to go about making GE successful. He is all about gaining competitive advantages through a deeper understanding of business ecology than a competitor. If there was one lesson to be taken away from this chapter, that is it.

Which leads to the subject of knowledge management, better known as KM. It is a field that has been studied by academics for decades, but only began to draw the attention of business managers and business school professors beginning in the 1980s. The result is that at the end of the 1990s there was a rapidly growing body of knowledge about how best to apply KM while at the same time managers in the industrialized world were largely ignorant of the topic. If we are to manage as Jack Welch suggests, the gap has to be closed. What managers need to do is explored in Chapter Three, where I discuss the role of today's economic shock troops, knowledge workers.

ENDNOTES

1. For a massive collection of material on this topic see James W. Cortada and John A. Woods (eds.), *The Quality Yearbook* (New York: McGraw-Hill, 1995–present), published annually. Each edition is approximately 800 pages in length.

2. Alfred D. Chandler, Jr., research forthcoming in print.

3. Two books that most triggered recent interest in the subject are *Intelligent Enterprise: A Knowledge and Service Based Paradigm for Industry* by James Brian Quinn (New York: Free Press, 1992) and *Competence-Based Competition* by Gary Hamel and A. Heene (New York: John Wiley & Sons, 1994).

4. IBM has acquired a very deep competency in IT services and related consulting. In fact, in 1999, over a third of the company's

(New York: McGraw-Hill, 1993), *TQM for Information Systems Management* (New York: McGraw-Hill, 1995), and with John A. Woods, *Qualitrends* (New York: McGraw-Hill, 1996).

12. Robert E. Cole, *Managing Quality Fads: How American Business Learned to Play the Quality Game* (New York: Oxford University Press and Milwaukee: ASQ Press, 1998): 227–232.

13. Dennis Bengston and Eric Lesser, "Turbocharging Business Processes with Knowledge," *Journal of Innovative Management* 4, no. 1 (Fall 1998), reprinted in James W. Cortada and John A. Woods (eds.), *The Knowledge Management Yearbook 1999–2000* (Boston: Butterworth-Heinemann, 1999): 367–378.

14. For example, H. James Harrington and James S. Harrington, *Total Improvement Management: The Next Generation in Performance Improvement* (New York: McGraw-Hill, 1994) and Brian Joiner, *Fourth Generation Management: The New Business Consciousness* (New York: McGraw-Hill, 1994).

15. Harvey Thompson, *The Customer Centered Enterprise* (New York: McGraw-Hill, 2000): 5–19.

16. Admittedly an extreme example, it makes the point. In its last five hundred years it embraced Christianity, broke up into two empires (West and East, one headquartered in Rome, the other in Constantinople), and gave up over 50 percent of its territory. Ultimately, the eastern variant of the empire lasted until the Renaissance. But this case illustrates how organizations will evolve to survive.

17. Eugene Marlow and Patricia O'Connor Wilson, *The Breakdown of Hierarchy: Communicating in the Evolving Workplace* (Boston: Butterworth-Heinemann, 1997) is a thoroughly up-to-date review of the subject as applied to the kinds of organizations discussed in the book you are reading. Because of the increasingly global nature of business, communications practices have international implications, well introduced by S. Paul Verluyten, "Business Communication and Intercultural Communication in Europe: The State of the Art," *Business Communication Quarterly* 60, no. 2 (June 1997): 135–143.

18. One of the clearest explanations to appear in recent years on how this is the case is by Joiner, *Fourth Generation Management,* 101–178.

19. Professor JoAnne Yates at the Sloan Business School at MIT has been studying the insurance industry and is preparing a ma-

about the implications for management today. An excellent example of applying a social science or humanities discipline is the use of cultural anthropology to understand consumer behavior. For an introduction to how this is done, see Paco Underhill *Why We Buy: The Science of Shopping* (New York: Simon & Schuster, 1999): 11–39.

26. Doug Garr, *IBM Redux: Lou Gerstner and the Business Turnaround of the Decade* (New York: HarperBusiness, 1999) and Robert Slater, *Saving Big Blue: Leadership Lessons and Turnaround Tactics of IBM's Lou Gerstner* (New York: McGraw-Hill, 1999).

WHO ARE THESE
KNOWLEDGE
WORKERS?

*Leave my factories but take away my people
and soon grass will grow on my factory floors.
Take my factories, but leave my people, and
soon we will have new and better plants.*

ANDREW CARNEGIE, 1889

A manager of a logistics process in an automobile tire manufacturing plant is doing knowledge work when he ponders how to eliminate a bottleneck in moving products from inventory to trucks late in the week. He may be looking at data on timing of deliveries, considering on-time delivery trends, and analyzing which truckers are involved. The professor observing and thinking about the significance of a molecular structure is also doing knowledge work. So is the police officer who, on a hunch, thinks he knows where a stolen car might be found. The CEO pondering a possible strategy decides to have dinner with a partial competitor to discuss "things." Knowledge work grows out of the series of tasks that require processing of information to take some action. Increasingly, this activity characterizes pieces of work and even whole jobs. Knowledge is valuable.

have to catch up with what managers have learned about the topic and how best to understand its value.[3] Knowledge workers are a key component to that new understanding, and more important, will be the source of much new wealth and profit in the early years of the twenty-first century. Make no mistake about that. As a result, we have no choice but to understand knowledge work and how to leverage it for profit.

INTRODUCING FAMILIAR ROLES AND NEW FUNCTIONS

Knowledge work can be described in essentially three ways. First, it is work of a cerebral nature, such as teaching, that has been around for a very long time. Second, managers usually see it as work of recent origin, such as management and consulting, both new jobs since the mid-nineteenth century. Third, and less visible, it is the incremental rise in knowledge content in work one never thought about before, for example, the use of information and insight coupled to a laptop computer by a construction foreman. But wrapped around all three types of roles is the growing recognition that there is such a thing as knowledge work. That recognition is itself a part of knowledge work.

Let's deal with the knowledge work of long standing because it has economic value and increasingly occupies a greater part of the emerging economy. The traditional pools of knowledge workers resided largely in the public sector, as teachers, lawyers, judges, lawmakers, government clerks, researchers, and professors at universities. They also expanded in number in highly industrialized economies. Historically, religions also provided a nurturing environment for knowledge workers that included priests, teachers, healers (today doctors). The roles of such people secularized increasingly into nonreligious professions, such as those of counselors, scholars, and the medical profession at large. Much of this evolution occurred during the twentieth century. The process of secularization of knowledge work continues. For example, in the United States, home to a

time that allegiance to the individual's profession or body of knowledge increased, making it easier for an individual to move from one firm to another without the emotional pain he or she might have experienced in the 1970s or the 1980s. In that earlier time, allegiance to an organization was normally more important than allegiance to a person's profession. Third, those with stock options who would have been able to cash in part or all of them have acquired economic independence sufficient to allow them to seize control of their calendars as well. In short, there is a variety of reasons why an increasing number of highly skilled individuals are changing jobs, focusing more of their time on a knowledge-based specialty. Ultimately, those who are good at what they do are making a living, and are often remunerated better than if they were members of a large corporation. Many are reporting that they are experiencing enhanced quality of life, even if the days are long. This scenario is a relatively new phenomenon.

In addition to the role of people, there is an organizational dimension to knowledge, because enterprises have much information that can be used for profitable activities. Just as it is convenient to think of human knowledge as intensively tacit, one can think of organizational knowledge as extensively explicit. Examples of the explicit form of knowledge include facts, ideas, processes, and techniques that can be communicated, documented, and shared among employees and business partners. Often these forms of knowledge are collected, and hence made available to many, out of attempts to catalog and document tacit knowledge. These collections of both explicit and tacit knowledge are intended to provide common frameworks, language, shared information, and experiences for everyone in an enterprise. Often we call an organization's knowledge Intellectual Capital. One of the most popular forms of this body of knowledge is best practices, two others are intellectual capital and competencies.

Firms that leverage knowledge management for sound business reasons exploit tacit and explicit knowledge, creating the processes necessary to make the two interact effectively, while providing tools to facilitate that dialogue. The challenge is to cause each to grow in usefulness and currency. We see

of all large organizations (both public and private) over the past millennium, particularly in Western (Christian) cultures. Sixth, the collection of information has normally led to creation of knowledge and its use. Seventh, one can document people's increased respect for the value of information and knowledge.[5]

Knowing where knowledge workers come from helps us understand the value and role they play in today's economy. While this is not the place to provide a formal history of their evolution, what managers need to know is that the percentage of the workers in the industrialized world who devote their time to knowledge work increased sharply during the twentieth century. It was a long process, with significant increases in the number of knowledge workers in each decade, expanding steadily the percentage of the working population involved in knowledge work. In short, as industrial capitalism spread, along with the use of corporations and centralized governments, the need for knowledge work to do the tasks of these organizations expanded too. Again, there are patterns of behavior.[6]

First, we know that a class of knowledge work comes into existence when a body of related information has to be collected, applied, and built on for subsequent actions. This is where we run into the discussion about core competencies of an organization, paths of learning for both an enterprise and an industry, and, of course, the role of individual skills and experiences.

Second, management often creates knowledge work by introducing new knowledge handling technologies. It is one of those unintended consequences technologists often speak about, and it occurs because a new tool makes possible new uses of a technology. Initially, experts on transistors thought they would be used to improve hearing aids; instead they became the engines of computers of the 1950s and early 1960s. Invention of the typewriter led to the creation of the job of secretary as we know it today, opening up a career path for women not available to them before. Invention of the computer led to careers: programmers, systems analysts, IT con-

is increasing all over the world. Finally, we are seeing a very rapid increase in the use of proven ways of applying knowledge to generate profits in business or efficiencies and quality of performance in governments.

HOW ARE KNOWLEDGE WORKERS LEVERAGED TODAY?

In a word, poorly. After a decade of discussion about corporate core competencies, professors publishing on the subject of product innovations, and the investment of billions of dollars in computing, we still approach knowledge management as if it were a new, even strange, subfield of management. Yet the truth is, if you were to think about it for a few moments, you would have to conclude that how knowledge management is performed is not so different from many other business activities. To be sure, it has its own specifics, but then so do manufacturing, accounting, marketing, and distribution. But why the poor performance? Are there examples of how to do it right? Let's begin with evidence of poor performance, which is everywhere:

- Enormous investments in PCs that senior executives complain are not being used to create value
- Academic admonitions to apply KM to product innovations meet with little success
- Experts leaving firms because the company offers early retirement incentives to drive down operating costs
- Failure to leverage core competencies of the firm to grow revenues from new sources
- Insufficient familiarity with customer and market needs and wants

On the other hand, there are examples and patterns of positive practices overlooked by many. For instance, most biotechnology and small software start-up firms exploit tacit and explicit knowledge to create their offerings. They may not know that they are practicing knowledge management, but they are doing it. The fact that thousands of these firms exist,

One way to look at the management issues involved has been emerging at IBM since the mid-1990s, developed simultaneously as much by KM experts as by engineers, researchers, and line management in field organizations. Essentially it calls for thinking of KM as operating within a business ecology, which we can describe as an environment populated with enablers, inhibitors, and drivers. To the extent that we can leverage enablers, constrain inhibitors, and exploit drivers, we increase the chances of profitably leveraging knowledge.

The most obvious enabler today is the network, whether it is an internal telecommunications net or the Internet. Connections among many people and organizations represent a growing reality. This is an enabler that will grow in importance as people figure out how to use it to share information and get work done quickly and relatively inexpensively when compared to older, slower approaches. Deregulation of communications is now a worldwide trend, which means increased connections will become incrementally available to more groups of people around the world and exponentially in the richest economies. We are beginning to see technical standards appear that govern practice and technology in the Internet and with telephony, particularly affecting wireless communications (e.g., cell phones). This trend toward the use of standards will have the same effect of expanding connectivity and hence sharing of information and knowledge that common standards have had in the past in stimulating the use of telephones, TV, radio, and PCs. Network bandwidths are improving rapidly, which means individuals will be able to receive and send information faster and in many forms, such as in video and sound, both of which require enormous increases in cheap capacity within a network to be cost effective.

In fact, we are learning more about network computing as new software tools appear whose use require less knowledge about computers and telecommunications. These tools keep coming into so many markets, allowing us to share information and collaborate in ways easier and different than even in the late 1980s or early 1990s. Lotus Notes is an obvious example of the new tools, but talk to its developers and they will

regard for their skills or corporate heritage. Executives clothed the rationale for this action in arguments related to Wall Street pressures, need for profit, and organizational weight loss, or as evidence of strong senior management leadership. Often those expelled from firms were older workers, those who commanded the highest salaries within their levels and positions, but who also had the greatest amount of tacit knowledge stored in their brains. Many employees with minimal seniority left too, pushed out the door along with their vital technical skills and energy. The process of downsizing was too frequently insufficiently selective, so both low and high performers left. Examples abound: engineers with 20+ years of experience in the aircraft manufacturing industry, senior secretaries in most industries, senior salesmen in insurance and computer sales, young technically savvy people who moved to what today are many of the Silicon Valley firms just outside of San Francisco. This is not the place to debate the virtues of what happened; it is enough to acknowledge that a great deal of tacit knowledge disappeared in the process.

Leadership is a culprit, however, and that fact cannot be ignored. Lack of commitment to the preservation of core competencies has the same effect it did when organizations failed to respond to the global move toward better-quality products in the 1980s and toward more process-centric management practices in the 1990s. The issue is well understood and need not detain us here. Ultimately, organizations do what management is willing to focus on, even at the long-term expense of the enterprise's health.

Because knowledge management is so intimately tied to corporate culture, it cannot be ignored as an issue, both as an enabler and as an inhibitor. On the negative side, the issue of cultural influence on behavior usually centers on the problem of resistance to sharing information or to creating the infrastructure required to exploit knowledge. An obvious trap is for one part of an organization to create a KM infrastructure— such as an intellectual capital system—but then either block other parts of an enterprise from using it, or fail to encourage others to tap into it. Where such systems are exploited well, you can see the inhibitor's flip side. For example, major auto-

firm to manage the use of KM—a push approach—effective for specific business initiatives. Table 3.1 documents the advantages and disadvantages of each.

TABLE 3.1 Advantages and Disadvantages of Various KM Approaches

TYPE	ADVANTAGES	DISADVANTAGES
Gatekeeper	Results in structure, high quality, highly secure system.	Can be biased, can lead to creation of Knowledge Police.
Free-for-all	Easy access facilitating creation of grassroots knowledge databases.	Could lead to messy, unstructured systems with much data and little value.
Hub	Makes it possible for communities of practice to be islands of expertise while organizations change.	Complexity and amount of required participation very costly to smaller organizations.

SOURCE: *IBM Consulting Group, © 1998.*

So many managers have attempted to introduce KM practices into their firms that we are now able to collect some worst *bad practices*! Here are a few:

- Creating inflexible knowledge organizations constraining grassroots K-based activities
- Organizing knowledge by business units, rather than allowing cross-functional KM development and use
- Constraining the flow into one's organization of outside knowledge needed to avoid incestuous thinking that avoids realities of the marketplace

These are not technical issues for a company's chief information officer (CIO) to deal with. They are corporate cultural issues, the heart of management practices, and squarely the responsibility of all senior executives. A leading expert on knowledge management, Laurence Prusak, nails it on the head when he argues that "culture trumps everything." It is management's job to manage the creation of a KM-friendly corpo-

work. Identifying knowledge gaps in a firm occasionally leads to an acquisition to plug a knowledge hole. Other benefits exist, but these are the ones most commonly evident.

As with anything relatively new in an enterprise, some KM goes on with or without conscious effort. In other words, it is already there by accident and, therefore, when a manager begins to focus on KM, he or she can come to it from a variety of entry points. Figure 3–2, which is used by IBM consultants to determine where a firm is entering the KM game, illustrates the variety involved. What we know is that most firms experience some or many of these various stages of evolution. At the lower left corner of the chart you see firms that have little knowledge or use it poorly. In those instances, managers have to inject enablers into the firm to stimulate activity. These enablers can be programs, incentives, pilot projects, and so forth. Those already in the middle part of the chart often have cultural problems that need fixing, such as poor teamwork, ineffective use of information technology, or lack of conscious management skills. As firms move up this value chain in using knowledge for business advantages, cultural transformations are already profoundly driving KM. They probably could use more help on soft cultural issues and need to apply many of the tools and techniques of a learning organization. Those who ultimately rely on knowledge to extend their market reach, as through alliances and partnerships, struggle with the issues of creating a shared vision of which business objectives to achieve and how to create economic value for all involved, because much of this effort is covering new ground.

Effective knowledge management programs anywhere along the spectrum displayed in Figure 3–1 require a holistic approach, reaching from the business drivers (motives) just discussed to a well-articulated vision of what shareholder values management is trying to generate. Examples of what kinds of specific initiatives are needed abound. Some are displayed in Figure 3–2, where they are clustered around such issues as business drivers or shareholder value. Look at Communities of Practice—upper left corner—which helps satisfy several of the typical reasons for having KM, pictured in the upper left corner of Figure 3–2. These concern groups of employees with

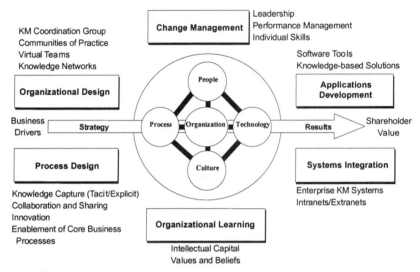

FIGURE 3–2
Effective KM Programs—A System View (Copyright © 2000 IBM Corporation)

holes, execute, then measure progress. There is no magic there; the specifics, however, can be unique. You can focus, for instance, on the problem of product or service innovations. In that case various groups within the firm may finally have to start working together that never did before. They would have to share common pools of information, databases on products, and market information. They now have to add to these repositories as they learn and work together. That whole process is often new to a firm embarking on KM.

Implementing a strategy for creating knowledge relevant to the enterprise is often also a new experience. Figure 3–3 provides a very simplistic, high-level representation of what such a strategy might look like. In this situation, the key notion to keep in mind is that you have to create a situation in which individual knowledge flows dynamically to other people, often using software tools (e.g., business intelligence systems, collaborative software such as groupware and e-mail, computer-based training, distance learning, database search tools, and corporate yellow pages). That leverages a growing and changing body of information owned by the organization as a whole.

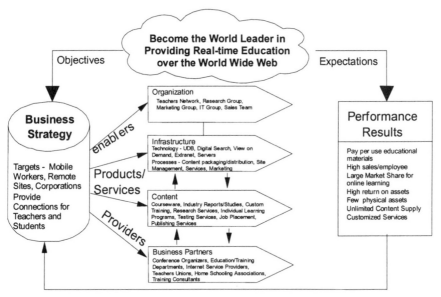

FIGURE 3–4
Example of a New Business Model Strategy (Copyright © 2000 IBM Corporation)

tion forms, data on filings and submissions, production schedules, shipping schedules, and inventory data. Suppose two out of four firms in the network are responsible for developing products. They would have to share information among groups of engineers, advertising, and marketing people from both firms, often accessing databases available to everyone involved. On the other hand, two other firms in the network might be responsible for delivery of products to the market, in which case they have to share information housed in databases regarding marketing, orders on hand, delivery schedules, and inventory data. That is knowledge management. Without it, the four firms would not be able to work together, make a profit, or extend their reach and scope in the market.

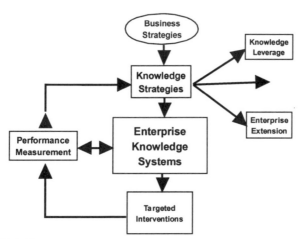

FIGURE 3–5
Overview of an e-KM Framework (Copyright © 2000 IBM Corporation)

capital. The point here, however, is that a KM strategy is injected into the model as a formal component.

Now look at the Enterprise Knowledge Systems. This refers to the installation and use of those tools and processes that make it possible to operationalize your knowledge strategy. It is here that organizational, cultural, and technological elements are systematically integrated. Business strategies and knowledge strategies are normally initiated by senior management, while the remaining components are the bread-and-butter activities of middle and lower management and KM teams. "Targeted interventions" is a fancy way of referring to those specific tactical activities that allow an organization to meet short-term objectives. In KM these can include such actions as conducting surveys, gathering data, building databases and yellow pages directories, training and coaching, or conducting scenario planning, modeling, and using expert systems. Much of what gets done occurs at this point, and the best normally have activities that deal with the sense and response activities of observing, gathering information, and forming assumptions about markets and opportunities. Second, these interventions concern the organization of information, from building contexts for workers (e.g., teaming behavior and use of technol-

What should be clear is that the e- here in KM is not just about pulling together a sales forecast for the quarter that integrates activities from around the world. Firms have been doing that for decades. It is about treating a global firm as if all its employees from around the world were located in one huge building, and all its customers in another building just down the street. Metaphorically that was always an ideal, never a reality. Today e- and e-KM make that metaphor a virtual reality. A company's operations can appear to be in one building and all customers in another, both nearby because of our growing ability to use technology and what we know about KM and process management to achieve the sorts of results once only dreamed about. That possibility is now being realized, and that fact is new. We could not accomplish this before the arrival of the Internet, software tools to manipulate information easily, and acceptance of process management as a reasonable way to organize work. Pockets of exceptions existed but they were just that, exceptions.

New value propositions are emerging. Take the bi-directional quality of any communications, in this instance the Internet. Priceline.com makes it possible for customers to bid for discount fares, hotel reservations, and even mortgages. In the elegant parlance of business management, Priceline.com is a reseller for airlines, hotels, and banks, charging a fee for bringing together customers and vendors in a mutually attractive arrangement. eBay provides an electronic auction house for people to sell just about anything. Millions have come to this firm, making it one of the most sensationally effective new companies to emerge that relies on the flow of information and use of the Internet. Even well-established bricks-and-mortar firms are finding opportunities. IBM sells intellectual capital via the Internet through its E-Business Accelerator (EBA). You can buy personal computers online from every major vendor. The "K" in all of these examples is the fact that the facilitating firm, e.g., Priceline.com or Dell, can collect information from the transactions going on, thereby learning what additional things to provide. Amazon.com, for instance, knows what topics I buy books on and, thus, routinely calls my attention to other volumes on the same subjects that I might want to con-

ple so often reach out to first, a few additional comments about technology are in order. The actions for management in regard to IT are essentially similar regardless of whether or not a KM strategy exists. However, without these actions taken within the context of a strategy, management has to rely on the accidental or serendipitous to occur to make KM productive. We know that using IT to facilitate implementation of a KM strategy moves an organization from accidental benefits to predictable results.

KM is now a recognized body of management practices that began as insights and activities of small groups, involving mostly public sector issues, such as those of government agencies, and in organizations that had significant prior experience with both IT and intellectual capital, such as consulting firms. Some, like the U.S. Department of Defense, supported development of IT tools that we have come to consider a natural evolution of commercial conditions, such as data mining and telecommunications. Nothing could be farther from the truth. Cost justifying a telecommunications network in business in the early 1950s was as easy as finding hen's teeth. It had never been done before. Next came applications in such areas as product design and development, followed by manufacturing, and, simultaneously, marketing. But not until the early 1990s did people even begin to use the phrase knowledge management.[8] Process management practices, for example, developed slowly all through the 1920s and 1930s under various names. They acquired statistical process control features in the 1950s and 1960s (largely thanks to J. Edwards Deming),[9] and became a mainstream activity first in Japan in the 1960s and then in the United States and in Western Europe in the 1980s and early 1990s. I would argue additionally, however, that process management is not evident across all parts of a commercial enterprise, mainly in evidence in manufacturing and engineering, despite the general use of the phrase "process management" by most departments. For that reason, we might also come to suspect that with KM we are paying more lip service to the term knowledge management than practicing its tenets.

ference rooms where they can meet. Walk though IBM's research labs in Yorktown, New York, and you will see people with beards coming to work at odd hours of the night and meeting in little alcoves that open onto a beautiful landscape. Go to any of IBM's multimedia centers and you will feel that you are in a movie studio; in fact, Emmys and Oscars stand on some credenzas! Go to a major consulting firm and you will see consultants working until late at night, with empty pizza boxes piled up in the hallway. Pick any profession that has knowledge workers and you see similar behavior: architects working on a Saturday and thinking it's fun; lawyers putting together a case, spending 70 hours a week doing it; Silicon Valley programmers moving from job to job if the working conditions are not just right, thirty-something CEOs of .coms living at work. Microsoft expects its people to work half days and, as the joke goes, they pick which 12 hours! Cokes are free, thanks to Bill Gates! So what is going on here? Knowledge workers either work because they have to or because they love their work. The more complex the knowledge work, the more satisfaction they get from what they do. Opinion surveys have borne this out for years. The biggest complaint is normally that their employer imposes on them bureaucracy and paper work, and does not provide the latest tools (I think for some, high-tech toys).

The point of this little diatribe is to indicate that as knowledge work increases, the role of management shifts from just leading in a direction to one in which they must create a fruitful environment and act as facilitators so that the "real work" of the enterprise can take place. Why do managers lend themselves to this? The short answer is that complex knowledge work calls for two things workers have: tacit knowledge and creativity. In the Information Age those assets are better than gold. Most CEOs have the same attributes—experience, tacit knowledge, and imagination—and that is why we pay them 8, 10, or more times as much as middle managers. Experience is the most important component of this formula. Relevant experience makes knowledge workers desirable, hence mobile. That is why a good movie production manager will tell you that the biggest challenge is making employees happy.

cally and as a set of tactical moves to help a manager or employee along. The list is short, but links neatly to what we know today about the effects of knowledge management. It also is a useful list to guide anyone in figuring out what technology is useful in support of KM.

Hire people with the right skills. It is a quick fix, costs less than inventing your own, and allows one to build on those bodies of knowledge needed to be competitive. The major downside is the risk that one runs of relying only on hired KM, in which case a firm cannot necessarily know more than a potential competitor because one's knowledge is held by others and becomes a relative commodity. Hiring people with the right skills does not mean recruiting folks who know how to use Microsoft Word, for instance, because people with that knowledge are everywhere, but rather employees who can contribute to the core competencies of one's organization.

Train, train, and train. In addition to people needing new specific skills (e.g., how to use a specific software tool), they need to learn more about their jobs, industries, and markets in ways that academics, philosophers, and career military personnel and others with insight do. Good managers appreciate that if a human being has various types of knowledge or information, they will create new insights and knowledge not thought about before. It is in that mental activity of formulating new insights that the promise of new products and services are realized, where new value chains are created. If these thoughts are followed by action, one does have new products, services, and opportunities for revenue. How much should a company invest in training? That question is difficult to answer; glib recommendations from trainers and HR managers range from four to six percent of budgets to two to three weeks for each person. However, those numbers are too absolute; it all depends on what training is needed and by whom. We know most people benefit from training, and that in an information and skill-intensified economy most, if not all of them, have to add constantly to their storehouse of information, skills, and knowledge. While training can only provide some of these enhancements, it is an important source.

ture. Walk into any company bragging about its intellectual capital and KM processes, and the first thing you will be shown is a computer and a demonstration of the massive databases built to house all this information. But usually the fact is that what you see is an expensive, although useful, electronic file cabinet. Like an old file cabinet filled with paper, it is not very useful unless one has knowledgeable people wisely using these files. For many firms that process begins with e-mail, online chat rooms, and competency databases. KM then seems to evolve closer to what the experts suggest, to changes in corporate culture that facilitate sharing of information, getting experts together fast to focus on specific issues, then gathering and analyzing data intelligently to improve processes and personal skills. It is a logical evolution, one that complements what happened in corporations between about 1880 and the start of World War II, when they and their office products suppliers used or invented file cabinets, three-ring binders, 3 x 5 cards, and most of the reports that business employees came to rely on during the first seven decades of the twentieth century as tools facilitating intracompany communications.[12]

Where the crucial IT investment has to be made is in collecting, delivering, and performing analysis on data deemed useful to knowledge workers. However, the use of technology itself is not knowledge management. That still is an activity primarily done in the human brain. That is why just installing e-mail or converting a twenty-year-old EDI system into some updated client-server transaction system is not enough.

CIOs and line management learned to deploy three basic strategies, however, that facilitate the activities of knowledge workers. First, management lets employees install tools they (the employees) deem useful so long as costs do not get out of hand or are impossible for the IT organization to support. Second, IT professionals then lash together these systems and tools through common technical standards which essentially remain open for anybody to use when they see it would make sense in their work. Third, management rewards and praises those who share information and leverage analytical tools to gain insights quickly about how to improve operations or generate new sources of revenue. As a codicil to good management

- Spreadsheet software that electronically draws down available data from internal databases and commercially available ones too

Make sure people know that these tools exist and provide training on their use. Finally, as the organization evolves into increasingly process-centric enterprises, make sure that information generated by the use of such tools is applied. Do the same if building a matrix management organization. It is not clear whether a traditional command-and-control corporate culture benefits as fully from the use of such tools, since implied in their application are empowered employees allowed to act on the insight they gain. Too much running to managers for direction or instructions makes the efficient application of KM problematic.

A second group of tools is technologies embedded in other machines and processes that can take feedback analogically and self adjust. For example, the computer chip designed to adjust fuel consumption in a car to optimize fuel efficiency represented a very early application. Today, hardly any major industrial equipment is without some self-adjusting intelligence. Large devices also self-report their patterns of behavior. At IBM since the early 1980s, medium and large computers have quietly been calling back to their factories of manufacture by telephone line to report performance occurring outside of design specifications, meaning out of the ordinary, for possible correction through electronic delivery of repairs. Large photocopiers today signal repair personnel that certain parts are malfunctioning. Another example is the Coca-Cola vending machines that signal their suppliers when they are empty. Operating systems in computers and copiers have been corrected by telephone for nearly two decades. When I plug into IBM's internal telecommunications network, the company simultaneously sends me updates to my installed software and often scans for viruses while I am doing what I consider to be my "real work."

"Sense and respond" systems represent a whole new class of applications with intelligence and feedback built into them. The term "sense and respond" has been in wide use within the

rapidly becoming less expensive, and with so much market data cost-effective and competitively priced by information suppliers, size has essentially been eliminated as a factor in whether or not to implement knowledge management practices. The tools are now cheap enough for all firms to use. Large, medium, and small companies all have to do the same things to leverage employee knowledge and institutional core competencies. The issues separating them are the ones that always differentiated firms: scale and scope. However, what is different today is the ability of all sizes and shapes of firms to use KM, to partner and form alliances, and to reach markets around the world through the use of such tools as the Internet and other forms of telecommunications. That is why a large firm like General Motors in the United States can work effectively with a small company with deep skills in Europe to design new components, or why a tiny firm in Hong Kong can hope to manufacture made-to-order goods for suppliers and jobbers in North America. As noted in earlier chapters, geography is no constraint to the activities of knowledge workers.

But there is more to work than knowledge management tools. Knowledge work is done within the context of work in general. The activities of work have been changing as the emerging Information Age economy has been developing. Therefore, understanding the emerging patterns of work in this new economy becomes a crucial body of knowledge for all managers. For that reason, in the next chapter I turn to an analysis of the changing nature of work.

ENDNOTES

1. Jorge Reina Schement and Terry Curtis, *Tendencies and Tensions of the Information Age: The Production and Distribution of Information in the United States* (New Brunswick, N.J.: Transaction Publishers, 1995): 21–39.

2. But computers are still blamed for loss of jobs. See, for example, Jeremy Rifkin, *The End of Work: The Decline of the Global Labor Force and the Dawn of the Post-Market Era* (New York: G.P. Putnam, 1995): 6–11, 101–106. Peter Cappelli et al., on the

11. The United Nations collects massive amounts of data each year, which it constantly publishes. Some of the useful series for the themes discussed in this chapter include the U.N.'s *Demographic Yearbook* (New York: UN, annual); but also see Organization for Economic Cooperation and Development's annual publication, *Employment Outlook* (Paris: OECD, annual).

12. For a fascinating history of these paper-based tools for preserving information and communicating, see JoAnne Yates, *Control Through Communication: The Rise of System in American Management* (Baltimore, Md: Johns Hopkins University Press, 1989).

13. Thomas H. Davenport, *Process Innovation: Reengineering Work Through Information Technology* (Boston: Harvard Business School Press, 1993) made the most widely read argument in support of this point.

14. Perhaps because of the size of the firm, there were some divisions that had done a better job than others exploiting IT and KM. The critical lesson: At least know what others in your firm have already learned and leverage that earlier experience and insight!

15. The topic has a growing body of best practices. See Stephen H. Haeckel, *Adaptive Enterprise: Creating and Leading Sense-and-Respond Organizations* (Boston: Harvard Business School Press, 1999).

CHANGING WORK: ROLE OF THE INTERNET

It is the interest of the commercial world that wealth should be found everywhere.

EDMUND BURKE

The research of many economists and students of modern work and society clearly demonstrates that work in the industrialized world is changing. There is no need to cover that ground again. What we need to discuss are those portions of the work of companies that are changing most as a direct result of an expanding global economy influenced by e-business activities. By work I mean not just the tasks of individuals—the usual definition of work—but the activities of organizations and teams of managers, especially executives, and also their employees.

But first a few realities. Much about work remains as it has been for a long time, perhaps with more technological help, but nonetheless similar. Hamburgers are cooked essentially the same way as in years past, dry cleaners use similar technologies and processes today as a decade ago, and taxes are

sizing to reduce overall expenses, a global company looks at such actions around the world, not just in one country, although senior management may elect to downsize only in one nation. But the point is that companies normally look at the total picture before making a decision.

At the same time as the classic industrial model of management is alive and well, with many forms of traditional work hardly modified or only slightly transformed by technology for instance, new elements are bearing down on the nature of work. Some of these have been discussed in earlier chapters. Many are profoundly significant. The one new element that is of greatest interest to management and the source of much curiosity, of course, is the role of the Internet.[2] As suggested earlier, it is an important consideration worthy of our attention, worry, and excitement. Because it is such an important new component in the work equation, we need to focus our attention on it. I describe some of the questions managers and employees are dealing with when figuring out how to mix work and the Internet to create competitive ways of generating profitable revenue. This chapter is, therefore, only a slice of the broad topic of work, but about the one of greatest importance at the moment, one that will probably continue to draw management's attention at least through the second decade of this new century. By then management should have worked out many of the uncertainties presented by the Internet for both the nature of work and the tasks of management.

THE ISSUE OF THE NET

The reason the Internet, or e-business, gets so much attention is because business people realize that this networked collection of technological innovations is changing many things so quickly that traditional activities in the physical economy are being displaced by this new situation. We know that enterprises are evolving when they use this technology for greater uses of collaboration and alliances. They rely on more knowledge work, mobile workforces, and rapid communica-

TABLE 4.1 Sample changes underway due to the exploitation of the Internet

PRE-INTERNET	POST-INTERNET
Brand issues are about physical products and services and how they are consumed.	Now the issues are about how customers select and use products online.
Relationships with customers are distant, often through stores and retailers.	Now customers contact manufacturers and services providers directly.
Brands stand for quality and reputation.	Brands stand for competence and trust.
Fixed prices or auction prices, vendor initiated.	All prices and terms are negotiable, customer initiated.
Cost of marketing varies.	Cost of marketing is more fixed.
Returns increase with scale.	Returns are based on type of scale.
Products and services turn over at predictable times, dictated by vendors.	Products and services turn over more often, dictated by customer wants.
Competition is fairly well understood and its sources well identified.	Competition is often new and non-traditional, and its sources less understood.
Markets are geographic and national.	Markets are global and continental.
Markets are subject to local government regulations and taxes.	Markets are subject to multiple governments and possibly simultaneously free of government interference.
Markets were limited to three dozen industrialized nations.	Markets are expanding to several dozen more nations, which are emerging with standards of living able to afford the Internet.

There are two pieces to the Internet story. The first involves that portion of the economy directly a part of the Internet, such as telecommunications, software developers, and businesses, providing service to users of the Internet. The

ized offerings, enterprises have to become very good at five kinds of transactional activities. They can be listed quickly:

- Efficient in maintaining and using distribution networks
- Efficient in moving information among all players in one's value chain
- Cost effective in conducting payment activities
- Running a well oiled supply chain as a process
- Coordinating logistics on behalf of one's customers

From a marketing perspective, requirements emerging today suggest what one has to be good at as well. These too can quickly be listed:

- Developing new services that enhance attractiveness and profitability of current offerings
- Exploiting computing and communications infrastructures regardless of who owns or operates them
- Offering new services at a profit

Our own research at IBM, and in particular the Watershed study, clearly demonstrates that management teams happy with their exploitation of e-commerce displayed strong capabilities in each of the two lists above. This insight suggests very strongly that these are good indicators of how firms are crafting their new value chains. From these features managers can design their own business architectures. Results are changes in three areas: a firm's value proposition (what is offered to customers), relationship management (how it deals with customers), and efficiency of the business (how cost-effectively, quickly, or accurately a company performs).

The hunt for new businesses in the e-business world is underway across most industries, with the result that there are many cases to emulate. Amazon.com is not the only instance, just one of the better known. Streamline uses telecommunications to automate its replenishment of groceries. American Airlines sells online highly discounted seats that might otherwise have gone unsold. Levi Strauss designs and makes customized blue jeans. Boeing uses technology to improve speed to market. In the area of new technology management approaches, we have the example of GE's Lighting

As this book was being written in late 1999 and early 2000, the IT press filled with stories about the concern companies had about security problems related to the Internet and wireless communications. The noise level generated by these issues was even louder in the popular press, particularly in the United States and in Western Europe, just as had been the commotion about potential Y2K problems in the first half of 1999. But, as with the Y2K concern, these were false issues because at the same time companies were installing effective encryption software within the Internet and across wireless telecommunications, most aggressively by retailers and financial institutions. Furthermore, quietly but effectively, companies created secured networks for internal use called intranets. These are internal systems available only to those authorized to use them, such as fellow employees accessing through company-issued passwords. So the problem of secure credit information or confidential documents, while irritating on occasion, was beginning to come under control.

The wireless telephone has an enormous future because it is far easier and less expensive to implement than laying down cable and wire networks. This has proven to be the case time and again throughout Africa and in parts of Asia and Latin America where governments could not afford wire-based infrastructures, let alone maintain them. Buy a phone, wireless phone, or a modem for a PC, and then rely on a U.S. company to maintain a network of communications satellites, and you have cheap access to the Net or to a national telephone network!

Another major technical consideration with the Internet is miniaturization and consolidation of hardware technologies, such as PCs and cell phones. For over a half century in the field of electronics we have observed a constant, relentless, yet effective move to make electronic devices smaller. The transistor, chip, and fiber optic cables all made profound contributions to this historic trend. Now we even see electromechanical machines being built that can only be seen through a microscope, with initial applications appearing in medicine and military drones. These machines are being equipped with instructions and continue to shrink. Small and smart, they

WHAT MAKES THE INTERNET DIFFERENT

What makes the Internet different is that work and opportunities change from those of the past, and often profoundly and swiftly. Take opportunities as an example. One type of change concerns the content or work and knowledge because information can be shared across the entire value chain quickly and cost effectively. Schwab provides its customers with a great deal of information about companies that they and other brokers used to charge for, with the result that customers can now do their own research and then place their own orders. Egghead Software began selling its products through the Internet, thereby eliminating the need for retail stores (roughly 80 percent of their employees) while providing information and services to their customers.

A second innovation touched on earlier in this book is the changing nature of commerce, where business-to-business transactions have increased and become more comprehensive via the Net. Now that initiative is being extended to customers. Then there is the third innovation, the collaboration made possible by easier-to-use software tools and the Internet to connect people and processes, employees to customers and to suppliers. We can expect more of these kinds of activities when they make sense. Will everyone rush to them? As I suggested in Chapter One, there is a fundamental change underway, sweeping across most industries at a fairly rapid rate. The only thing we do not know, however, is exactly how fast. It seems everyone is commenting on the topic, with most predicting rapid change, probably faster than it will occur. How fast is irrelevant anyway. Companies are reacting to the Internet and adopting its capabilities when it makes sense to their employees. If they guess wrong, competition bites them, move too early and they make mistakes. Move at a good clip, applying sound management practices, and a company arrives at a new way of making money.

Sound management practices include taking the experience you have with e-mail and networks and extending these to a larger pool of customers and suppliers, using the Internet

reinvent many of their offerings. Those that have done this include Bank One, Barnes and Noble, Charles Schwab, Cisco Systems, Dell Computer, IBM, and UPS. In short, the transformation cuts across many traditional industries. Other companies are born, the sorts of firms the University of Texas study suggested. Some of the better-known ones include Amazon.com, AOL, eBay, E*Trade, Yahoo!, and Priceline.com.

A third wave began emerging at the end of the 1990s, suggesting that even more profound changes await managers. In this phase, businesses are totally redesigned from top to bottom, while traditional organizational and industry boundaries dissolve. These changes lead to new bases of competition and obviously to new cost models. Everything seems very electronic. Figure 4–1 graphically illustrates the three waves. The learning point from this figure is that one can be at various

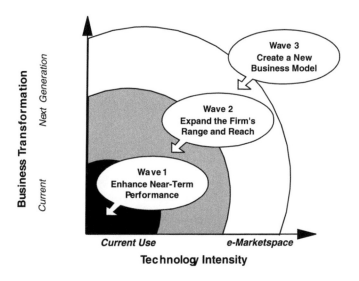

FIGURE 4–1
Waves of Business Transformation

stages of evolution.

The business literature about the Internet would suggest that everyone is somewhere deep in Wave 2 or 3. Nothing

ity to react to these, either to exploit opportunities or to minimize damage, will be essential. Understanding when these are occurring and then responding quickly are keys to effective performance. This involves more than just reading about trends and directions in the business press, it is the process of routinely gathering information about market conditions, changes in technology, and being a student of new uses of computing and the Internet. The problem is not the availability of such information, it is often the insufficient interest, especially of managers and thought leaders, to methodically be students of their environment with the boldness to take action based on what they are learning. Action by the prepared mind is essential in our current situation.

Third, access to markets is becoming crucial to any strategic positioning. This is a fancy way of saying that what markets a firm can get into becomes a critical influence on a firm's business strategy. The Internet's availability opens new doors. For example, the automotive industry is beginning to realize that additional sales of cars via bids and auctions from customers can offer incremental sales to either dealers or manufacturers. In the mid-1990s, the issue of the Internet turned on the question of whether dealers were becoming irrelevant and if so, what role (if any) they might play. So far, what has happened is that the need for dealers to sell cars still exists for those customers who do not want to bid on vehicles online; for those who do, dealers are still necessary as points to which customers can go to pick up their new vehicles, or get warranty repairs. That is a very different answer or set of opportunities than might have been conjured by the manufacturers in the mid-1990s. In this example, a market is being created made up of customers who want to buy via the Internet, either through some bidding process (the new emerging approach) or by carefully configuring exactly what they want online before haggling with a dealer (the approach most evident in the mid- to late 1990s). Today, the bidding approach is creating new opportunities, which in turn affects the marketing strategy and business plans of both manufacturers and dealers.

it captures information about what kind of PCs customers of its Web site try to configure)

■ Linking processes with suppliers and partners in other
regions, nations, and industries that can then be
extended out to your suppliers' and partners' customers,
thereby creating an additional pool of physical and electronic customers

While the foregoing list is skewed heavily to the creation of
incremental revenues, one can quickly come up with a similar
list to suggest how to drive down costs of operation. Some of
these have been mentioned elsewhere in this book, such as
the development of products using the Internet as a fundamental tool for collaboration with partners and multiple sites
around the world. Besides saving time and the cost of traveling
to each other, you can draw the ideal experts into a meeting
regardless of where they are and only for the amount of time
needed. E-mail, of course, remains the "killer app" that put
the Internet on the map in the first place.

Fifth, managers will spend more on IT than ever before,
and therefore, general managers will become even more fluent
in technological issues than in the past. This fluency will be
less about how gizmos work and more about the implications
of applied technologies. What it would mean to apply minia-
turized technologies, or combine two or more in new ways,
will be more important to them than simply using mainframes
to reduce backroom office applications or front office data collection. Whole new companies are being created, occupying
cracks that exist today between traditional industries (e.g., as
brokers of information and as agents combining services
together into new offerings).

Anyone working today in any role in any organization can
view the changes underway either defensively or offensively.
Most of the literature on the topic may frighten you, raising
questions such as:

■ How can we start making money by selling on the Internet?

■ To what extent can a competitor exploit our network to
capture our key customers?

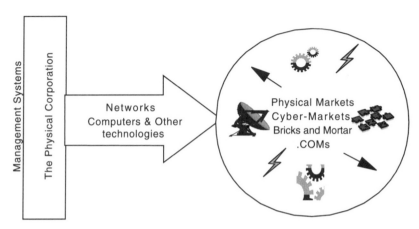

FIGURE 4–2
Managing in the New Markets

new markets and suppliers. Finally, there is the assortment of computers and other technologies that need to be strapped together in a cohesive manner to make the whole thing work.

By looking at networked-based environments, the management system required to function here, along with the business models that emerge, are all anchored to the market*space*. The description of that space becomes the basis for getting tactical about doing routine and familiar work. For each of these four areas, we can now ask some basic questions, the answers pointing to tasks to be done. Simply listed, they are:

- How is the environment changing? Related question, how does it affect my company?
- What should I do about it?
- How should I do it?
- With whom do I form alliances to get the work done?

The answers today are all over the place. But basic business management principles apply here just as they always did in other environments. Specifically in regard to the Internet, one still has to develop strategy, plan its implementation, build technical and business architectures, develop management practices and systems, construct networks and offerings, and run organizations.

products, services, and offerings (what we used to call unbundling) into various contexts, such as format, tone, logo, style, experience, or by content (e.g., product, services, information, even information-based products), and by infrastructure (e.g., business and IT processes or capabilities). In a desegregated world, you can do things in each of three areas or in only one or two, your choice. What influences the choice? Access to customers is a key influencer: ways or channels to reach customers and for them to gain access to your offerings and organization. A second involves the variety of products and services that the firm offers, the classic issue of mix. A third concerns what sets of customers to go after with ever more specific offerings. These three issues complicate yet enrich the opportunities presented through effective competition.

You can count on the process of learning how to use e-business to be an incremental iterative exercise, yet one that proves useful. Someone tries something, learns from that experience, and improves. The only admonition here is that this cycle must operate very quickly if it is to be effective in an e-business environment. Assemble a group of experts on networking and business and invariably they will come up with a similar list of insights and assumptions about working in an e-business environment. Here is a list from one group of experts in my firm:

- Market segmentation increasingly has to consider access as a secondary but necessary dimension of e-business.
- Electronic access increasingly is used by new entrants to easily and quickly cross industry boundaries.
- Currently available data mining tools and techniques are becoming drivers of new e-knowledge applications.
- Ability to support virtual communities will be required as a core competence of the firm, but it is valuable only if one can combine it with customer knowledge gathering (the sense and response issue combined with business intelligence).
- Generating revenue does not automatically mean enhancing margins now that context-based competition

of goods and services. That is why so many senior executives today are trying to understand the potential of technology in general, and specifically IT. Computers are creating great fissures along the formal boundaries of departments, companies, markets, and industries. The shifts, however, are occurring so far along existing lines when a manager separates information (usually data, not knowledge) from physical activity, usually thought of in terms of products and services. That is why the bulk of this chapter focuses on competition and marketing issues in the context of technology and, more specifically, the Internet.

Are there additional insights for management to gain by observing the three waves of change currently underway? Getting tactical is always important, and by now the reader has identified their firm with one of the three waves. Here is what we see going on with each.

In Wave 1, scope is typically intraenterprise, normally within existing supply chains and demand channels. Employees focus on streamlining existing work by leveraging technology. Three issues always face people at this point: prioritizing among a large collection of opportunities, ensuring strategic fit and initiatives that are complementary to the firm's strategy, and shutting down existing initiatives that now are out of synch with the overall strategy.

In Wave 2, scope typically expands to the whole enterprise or business unit, not just to a piece of it, and involves selected value nets. Life now becomes more complicated for managers as they face the prospect of making significant changes in processes, organization, and the deployment of computing technology. Managers also face the fundamental issue of how to manage existing work while moving to a radically different approach. We see this, for example, in managing channel conflict as a company, shifts from selling goods through dealers to selling through the Internet. How do you keep dealers happy and productive while they are getting mad at the fact that you are shifting to the Internet? Employees create new ways to perform tasks, learn different skills, and must adapt to changed working conditions. For most firms, Wave 2 is the

A SOBER VIEW OF THE FUTURE

E-business is real and will increase its share of commercial activity for the same reasons that steam, electricity, and other technological innovations did before. But it is important to put the Internet in perspective because press coverage of this technology has bordered on the ridiculous during the second half of the 1990s—filled with exaggerations, misinformation, and insufficiently grounded in the reality of how businesses work. An historical perspective gives us a more realistic, sober set of insights on the effect of this new technology on business practices. Such a view does not suggest that we are talking about things not changing, far from it, the transformation is robust.

The Internet, and its accompanying e-business applications, can be seen as an extension of a long process that began in the nineteenth century with the invention and rapid deployment of the telegraph and its vocal successor, the telephone. The reason the telegraph became so popular in the 1800s was its ability to deliver information rapidly across vast geographic space. What might have taken weeks to communicate now took seconds. Without this technology, as historians have long pointed out, creation of efficient railroad corporations in the United States and in Europe would have been delayed or never developed in their ultimate national scope. Deployment of the telephone, like the computer chip nearly a century later, created uses that were eventually replaced with new applications. As with the telegraph before it and the computer chip after, the telephone rapidly became a powerful tool in commerce with which to communicate information quickly across wide geographies. Over time, the cost of communicating via the telephone dropped sharply, as it continues to do today. The same occurred with use of computer chips. Thus, the telecommunications technologies of the past 150 years enhanced the ability of managers to extend their flow of information and simultaneously increased their ability to control commercial activities, most notably operations of corporations. In each instance in the evolution of telecommunications

Net and existing prior to the availability of this tool. Characteristics of e-business made unique by today's technologies and those that will come, have and will cause shifts in use; we see that with Wave 3 firms for instance. Such shifts will define the work of enterprises and the nature of their configuration. As with previous technologies, the effects are being felt first by large enterprises and by early alert new entrants into markets relying largely on the technology. If the past is any guide, then we can expect the technology to evolve to reflect the priorities and values of management teams aggregated across national economies and not solely by the realities of physics and electronics. Individual corporate uses will also reflect how they run today and tomorrow. Change will come incrementally yet very rapidly. These changes will appear cataclysmic and rapid to those involved. Historically, they will come to be seen as evolutionary over many decades.

I am pointing out these issues because a great failing of management in general (but their key employees too) is their lack of historical perspective. In the area of computers and networking, historical perspective is even more minuscule. Institutional memories are very weak due to the turnover of IT professionals, their relative youth, and the normal lack of sound knowledge management practices both in IT organizations and across the firms that own them. But let there be no mistake about it, all these technologies and their applications and consequences have a history that go back many years. One of the leading historians of the Internet, Arthur L. Norberg, has shown how the evolution of networking in the U.S. was closely linked to the transformation of earlier technologies and uses among government, academic, and business organizations.[9] It is the nature of corporate capitalism, set within the context of economies that generally (but not always) supported free trade and minimal government intervention, that made it possible for the vital interactions among technologies, management practices and values, and realities of the market place. It is that set of influences that affects the traditional tasks of management in the Information Age and cuts across the type and volume of resources, processes, and technologies.

historic trend of miniaturization made it possible to increase the amount of intelligence one could hang onto a telecommunications system, thanks to chips, lower costs, and a deeper understanding of how multiple technologies work together. Engineers move from one firm to another—as we are seeing with Silicon Valley programmers—and they read each other's technical literature. So exploitation of technologies is occurring very rapidly within a business and technical culture that embraces the belief that such change has to be constant and urgent[12]

We can realistically expect that the mixing and matching of technologies, which results in new products and applications, will continue for a very long time because most developers believe they are at the threshold of what they are doing. They are right to believe this because the merger of technologies is often going on for the first time, so maturity in that process has yet to occur. The Internet is an excellent example, but so are all the handheld devices (e.g., PCs and cell phones) just now being linked together. If you have any doubts about the scope of this trend, attend any one of the major computer trade shows, such as COMDEX in the United States, where, using this case, some 20,000 people see thousands of products *that did not exist a year earlier.* That show reflects the products of only one industry! Other high-tech industries, such as industrial equipment manufacturers, telecommunications, and even book publishers, are porting into their products computer components too.

This extensive mixing and matching means that firms will have opportunities, problems, challenges, successes, failures, and rapid change for some time. When these bursts of technological innovation occurred in the past, such as with the development of steam-driven machines in the eighteenth century, and later, with the introduction of electricity and modern chemistry in the nineteenth, it took well over a half century for these to play out sufficiently for businesses to understand the full implications of what was happening. Then it still took additional time for businesses to exploit fully the technological changes that came along. But what is grounded hard in historical reality is the fact that technological changes had a direct,

The second requirement is that everyone apply process management and knowledge management techniques and practices to organize their work, and that of their enterprises, in ways that ensure that intelligent transformations occur in a timely fashion.

Balance ultimately is what is required. Yes, the Internet and e-business are important. Yes, you will do more electronically than in the past. But these are tools to do the fundamental work of business, which is to develop products and services, sell them to customers, and do all over again, always at a profit. The tasks of businesses, such as strategy, training, selling, marketing, manufacturing, and so on, remain the common elements in the equation. Technology can dominate or, as proposed in this book, managers can leash it to their will. The Internet represents a wonderful new tool for facilitating the fundamentals of work. That is why it has become so attractive to businesses, government agencies, and individuals. We should not lose sight of this obvious fact.

Keeping that in mind is crucial as we now turn our attention to the issue of supply chains and value nets. These have been profoundly affected by the sorts of technologies discussed in this chapter. But they are also examples of how technology can be exploited by managers to do the historic work of businesses. Once again, we will see those immutable laws of sound economics and good management are alive and well.

ENDNOTES

1. Paul Osterman, *Securing Prosperity* (Princeton, N.J.: Princeton University Press, 1999): 90–115.

2. Numerous studies and surveys, from such organizations as the Conference Board, to business journals, such as the *Harvard Business Review*, have demonstrated this fact, beginning in the mid-1990s.

3. Carl Shapiro and Hal R. Varian, *Information Rules: A Strategic Guide to the Network Economy* (Boston: Harvard Business School Press, 1998).

18th Century) (Berkeley: University of California Press, 1992).

14. I had the great fortune of asking Braudel if his "follow the money" advice also applied to basic technologies, such as metallurgy, electricity, and computers, and he said it did. Interview, Baltimore, Md., April 1976.

Digitizing Supply and Value Chains

*Great things are not done by impulse, but by a
series of small things brought together.*

Vincent Van Gogh

Beginning in the 1960s, a profound revolution began in
the way management distributed work. What we began to see
was a significant increase in the interplay of technology with
work in general and with the actions and decisions of managers. Because this interplay increased so sharply—thanks to the
rapid deployment of computers—we can speak of a revolution
taking place. This revolution, like its political variant, started
with quiet root causes without a great deal of noise or people
shouting in the streets. As with so many other profound
changes that came in the second half of the twentieth century,
this transformation grew out of technological innovations and
their refinement. In this case the technological innovation was
online computing. Until the early 1960s, people fed work to
computers in batch jobs, bunches of cards handed to an operator through a window at a data center, and when enough of

by the early 1990s, to customers who could directly enter inquiries and orders into a vendor's computer without the supplier having to bear the expense of handling the work now off-loaded onto customers. By the mid-1990s, managers were aware of new potentials, grounded in prior experiences with distributed processing and telecommunications. They recognized the compelling attractiveness of expanding markets to a global stage. That set of experiences made them recognize relatively quickly after the World Wide Web was introduced that the Internet presented profound opportunities for new business models and incremental revenues, not to mention whole new lines of business and operational efficiencies.

An example of the dynamic nature of this phenomenon is the experience of UPS. When this company first made Internet tracking available in 1995, it received 100,000 tracking requests in December. By 1996 UPS saw over a million requests in December, and by December 1997, a million requests in a week. By 1998 that volume increased to a million in one day, and on December 21, 1999, UPS experienced 3.3 millions "hits" to its tracking system in one day. One can imagine the army of customer service representatives that would have been required to field that number of inquiries and the costs that UPS avoided by providing customers access to their shipment information.

It is not difficult to realize, then, that with such experiences companies increasingly pushed for greater links between technology and strategy, which is why by the end of the 1990s senior general executives wanted to know more about the potentials of information technology and, of course, about the Internet.

This chapter is about their growing awareness as it plays out in what many are conveniently calling supply chain management (SCM). The transformation of organizations and management practices to account for SCM is emerging as new paths to new value chains, and ultimately to the new value propositions discussed in Chapter One.

The reason for paying attention to supply chain management practices is straightforward: Many companies and cus-

THE VALUE OF VIEWING EVERYTHING AS A SUPPLY CHAIN

To begin with, we need a working definition of SCM because its definition varies depending on which constituency discusses it. Supply chains have also become increasingly larger, encompassing more aspects of an organization's work as it became more possible to do so. Before exploring SCM, managers and workers in the Information Age have to face a basic problem with the subject, namely, coming to an agreement about what it is because SCM is currently changing so rapidly in scope and form. For my purposes in this chapter, I define SCM as the activity that links and optimizes the processes, tasks, technologies, and terms of operation necessary to design, acquire components, and bring a product to market, to sell and deliver it, and to service it. The flow from one end to the other of such a supply chain can also involve just a service, such as dry cleaning or mailroom management. The origin of SCM came from managers breaking down the walls of highly optimized functional silos, such as sourcing, warehousing, transportation, and manufacturing, to manage the linked processes for an optimized result across the chain. The concept implicitly included the idea of sharing information about the logistics of raw material to finished products among all handlers. For example, Ford Motor Company can tell its tire suppliers what cars it will build next week, allowing suppliers to look at the production database in a Ford computer system to know what kinds of tires to deliver each day next week. The concept expanded to include backward forecasting, that is to say, retailers or customers telling vendors and suppliers what they thought they needed.

If this sounds very much like the electronic data interchange (EDI) of the 1970s and 1980s, it is because EDI taught participants in SCM about the value of information shared across multiple enterprises using telecommunications and computers, particularly in manufacturing industries. EDI and the sharing of information and knowledge facilitated the expanded use of SCM. Its consequences for how organizations

Third, a generation of managers and their staffs now have experience with process management practices, a crucial ingredient in the development of coordinated activities across multiple departments and enterprises. Put another way, a company cannot have supply chains across multiple organizations operating as sporadic activities. They have to be processes because of the high degree of coordination required to make them work. This means managing activities with the rigors that come from process management and organizing one's organization (people and assets) around such processes. Structured activities become the name of the game for all the same reasons that common language, legal practices, and predictable government policies were always crucial to the successful operation of "for profit" enterprises and capitalist economies. Certainty, predictability, and repeatability are hidden features essential to the effective functioning of processes.

Six features of economic activity have compelled firms to pay more attention to SCM than ever before. First, consumers acquired more power in the 1990s, demanding specific goods and services as a result of their increased purchasing capabilities and access to knowledge about these. As with some of the other features of the economy, use of the Internet stimulated these changes. As a result of this shift in power, we moved toward a pull approach to selling goods, making it attractive for customers to come to vendors. Second, already mentioned in this book, but appropriate to consider again at this point, is the historic shift from mass marketing to mass customization. This shift required more electronic transactions than ever (e.g., purchasing, coordinated manufacturing, and delivery), leading to fewer physical activities per sale (e.g., building and shipping products to stores, then again to customers). Third, markets became geographically larger as firms crossed international boundaries to sell to new sets of customers. Many business professionals refer to this as globalization, but in practice it is more a matter of building the capability to reach new customers with messages and offerings across a larger land mass, either within a domestic market or across national borders.

- A study by Pittiglio Rabin Todd & McGrath demonstrated that firms with effective supply chain management processes yield an average of 7 percent cost advantage and a 40 to 65 percent advantage in cash-to-cash cycle times over less effective firms. And, of course, such firms hold on to 50 to 80 percent less inventory, in itself another major source of economic benefit.
- A study by IBM and the *Financial Times* demonstrated that manufacturing firms could cut as much as 60 percent of their procurement staffs or improve availability of stock stocks by several percent without additional inventory costs.

What experts will tell you is that SCM processes go in faster than Enterprise Resource Planning (ERP) approaches, often in less than one year, frequently building on existing EDI-like infrastructures already familiar to trading partners. One can, for example, construct SCM processes with little or no dependence on such massive projects as ERP implementations. One can roll out new franchises to gain economies of scale. One can use SCM to create industry standards, as was necessary, for example, in the banking industry in the 1950s when it became one of the first to create industry-wide EDI practices for the exchange of money.

Studies and work done by IBM's own consultants, working with clients implementing both SCM processes and the technological infrastructures that underpin these, demonstrated the possible kinds of economic benefits firms were beginning to harvest. For example:

IN THE AREA OF COST SAVINGS:

- Reduced inventory levels ranging from 10 to 50 percent (consistent with historic orders of magnitude seen with the original round of EDI implementations in the 1970s)
- Reduced markdowns and scrap of 40 to 50 percent (a bit higher than when companies reengineered their manufacturing processes in the 1970s and 1980s with Deming's quality management practices)

Are there any rules of the road emerging on how to get this done? Veterans of the process speak about understanding the positive impact that changes in one's supply chain management processes have on their competitiveness. It is not simply an issue of lowering costs and improving customer service. Those experienced with SCM have found that there is a counterintuitive "virtuous cycle" that occurs when inventory is taken out of a supply chain. In order to function, process and quality have to improve, collaborations with trading partners and customers rule improvements, and speed becomes critical. When properly done, the results are lower costs, higher customer service, fewer writeoffs, and fewer assets required for a given level of sales.

Second, it is increasingly becoming evident that execution and decision making must be tightly coupled with all involved trading partners to ensure that the whole works as desired. In recent years Dell Computer has become a classic example of this at work. However, increasingly, other firms have learned to link execution and decision making. To a large extent, the decision of some .com firms to expand to additional offerings emerged out of such a linkage. The capability, for example, of Wal-Mart or Amazon.com to play on the Net are clear examples.

Third, senior executives point out that SCM does, just like ERP, fundamentally change how many tasks are performed. The effects on policies, practices, and internal politics is nothing less than profound. The cases of Amazon.com, eBay, and Priceline.com come to mind as modern examples of this phenomenon at work. In short, what we are learning about ERP implementations applies to SCM, even though the latter go in much quicker than the former because managers tend to implement them in piecemeal fashion. A piecemeal approach is not possible with most ERP software tools, where so many elements are integrated by design within their software packages by the vendors who sell them.

By definition, supply chains increase in value as they expand, becoming increasingly comprehensive and reaching more customers. That is why I argue that everything manage-

just to remain relatively competitive and profitable? The answer to this question varies by industry and company. The answers are not obvious or assumable because circumstances can change, often rapidly, as I suggested in the first two chapters of this book. When Ford and GM both announced on the same day that they were going to convert their procurement processes rapidly to Internet-based trading hubs, they changed the future shape of thousands of suppliers' supply processes in one bold stroke. So managers have to constantly ask the question and not be surprised if the answer keeps changing. The question is an excellent one to ask of an existing bricks-and-mortar firm, although increasingly it is the sort of question that drives a creative entrepreneur to a venture capitalist because of first entrant opportunities. People serving as brokers—intermediaries—in the world of e-commerce, for example, fit into this latter category. They can operate only if they have a supply chain built around what they do. Dell does not manufacture personal computers, but commissions others to do so, even making IBM part of its SCM process because of the components built by Big Blue. Intermediaries sell insurance online, making mainline insurance companies providers of insurance to customers brought to them via the Internet, often leading to rapid consolidations of market share in the hands of a few entrepreneurs.

4. What technical capabilities and infrastructure does one need to pull it off? The underlying message is that technical wherewithal is often more crucial today than the rationale for SCM. Putting all the technical pieces together is daunting, even for a large multinational corporation with its army of computer and telecommunications experts. Managers often outsource some technical functions because building one's own proves too expensive or too slow to accomplish. Increasingly, they also find they must either concentrate their energies on industry-specific capabilities or go buy those as well so that they can expand into markets otherwise closed to them. Partners and candidates for mergers and acquisitions are often chosen in part because of their technical capabilities and the information technology infrastructures they already have in place.

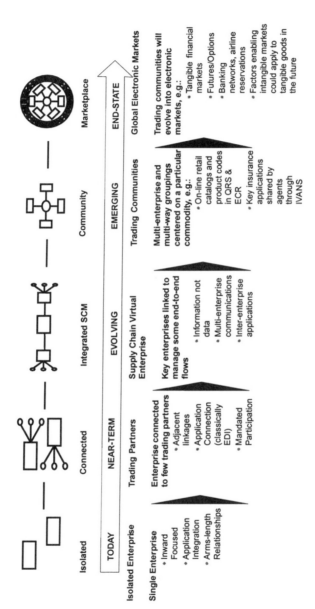

FIGURE 5-1
Evolving Supply Chains

From the start of the 1970s and continuing through the early 1990s, firms usually had a dedicated technical infrastructure with private networks. Today, a company is more likely to have a network that is the Internet with shared global networks. Prior to the 1980s, most firms did not share a great deal of electronically based information outside the walls of the enterprise. When a firm did share, it was most often with suppliers and always at some great expense, usually a third party or Value Added Network (VAN); networks were not cheap to build or maintain. Today, information is shared with whomever it makes sense to share it with, on a global basis, yet with controls over whom the firm authorizes to participate in access to its electronic files. Teaming used to be intracompany, with outsiders difficult to manage. The same was true for teams made up of employees from the same firm scattered around the country or world. Today, intracompany teams are very common, along with others made up of employees from widely dispersed geographic locations within the enterprise, following the flow of information, and coming in and out of departments more frequently than in the past. Control over who had access to a corporate network used to be physical or through passwords on internal systems. Today, an individual is given permission to access, shares information via authorization, and uses complex security systems to constrain who has access to sensitive data. Process management used to be a question of all process participants sitting around a table to discuss whatever issue was on the agenda. Today, you see such things as virtual product modeling, simultaneous engineering on a global basis, groupware for collaboration, and now effective video conferencing, Internet hookups for voice, combined video and text, and the use of such IT tools as Lotus Notes. They work, they are cheap, and people increasingly like them.

I suggested earlier that the world was changing; this is a good place to remember where and how. The Internet has a direct influence on any SCM in five areas: globalization, digitalization, compression of time and space, convergence of everything from products to industries, and empowerment of employees and customers. We do not need to cover this ground again. However, we do need to keep in mind that the Internet

percent, or more of their value during April and May 2000—investors lost faith that many new firms would turn a profit in a timely fashion. It is almost impossible to envision a time when profit would not be the ultimate measure of a business's success.

Given the reality of profit, what does managing and working in the Information Age mean? Adrian Slywotzky has spent as much time as anybody looking at this question, and he argues that we will need to know how people make money in our companies and in our industries. We still need to know where profit zones exist in our firms and markets. We must still design processes that concentrate on generating profits where markets allow a business to profit in the new Digital Economy. His perspective makes good sense because it is a callback to a time honored business reality.[2] Slywotzky argues that value migrates within industries. In the computer industry, for example, for many decades patterns of profit generation were linear, then they shifted. Instead of growing profits by selling either more profitable machines or additional quantities of them, profits shifted to software and hardware becoming less profitable. That is how we got Microsoft, today valued more by the marketplace than General Motors. As profitable products of the past became unprofitable, value migration was at work. In short, the source of profit moves on to some other part of the business or industry. For IBM in the 1970s, computers were THE source of all its profits. By the end of the 1990s, the firm's annual reports documented that the primary sources of profit were services and software. Value migration occurs in all industries, especially those experiencing rapid change. In fact, rapid changes are really sources of profits migrating to new points. Technology often causes or accelerates value migration. In other words, this migration results from doing all the things discussed in this book.

The challenge for management looking for value (profits) is less a question of designing a Porteresque value chain than it is building an organization that can quickly understand where profits can be had, how, and move there. No-profit zones within firms, markets, and industries are expanding, particularly in traditional forms of business where the impact of

owning some theaters, and licensing products and movies. High-tech companies, such as IBM, Intel, and Dell, make money by constantly introducing new products, building and delivering them cost effectively and fast, and then starting the process all over again. Speed and efficiency are crucial sources of profits for these firms. Their use of information and SCM practices is different than one might expect at Coca Cola, Pepsi, or Disney. GE started by wanting to be #1 in market share (the original Jack Welch strategy to making profits in a manufacturing firm), adding services, quality, and e-business to support share with productivity. GE did what IBM and so many others had. GE executives looked at their entire range of activities and offerings, taking a holistic approach. They sold products but also services wrapped around them. The services' piece of the equation increasingly became more profitable for all these firms. The moral of the story: Reconfiguration of value chains using SCM is occurring in all businesses and industries, offering every business team the opportunity to improve profit performance.

But within each industry and business, the actions firms need to take vary at both strategic and tactical levels, and these change over time. This is what happened at IBM, Coca-Cola, and GE. Managers, therefore, constantly have to ask themselves several questions as a routine part of building their business strategy. Even the .coms are not immune to this requirement. For example, both eBay and Amazon.com expanded and changed their offerings in 1999 to remain competitive. Simply listed, the questions that must be asked are:

- How do I make money (profit) today? Really? Are you sure?
- How is that changing (and, oh yes, it is changing whether you see it or not)?
- To what extent is my firm organized to support today's profit model and capable of shifting quickly to a new one?
- What does tomorrow's model appear to be? How do I align my resources to optimize that sooner than my competitors?

tion of the value proposition every few years as routine management activity is the message.

This notion of reinvention is a difficult one to implement, and so it is not always the most popular item on a manager's agenda. The notion is far from new. Business gurus and economists have to remind us of that fact every generation. However, let's acknowledge one of the most important original sources of this discussion, economist Joseph A. Schumpeter (1883–1950). An Austrian professor by birth and training, he joined the faculty at Harvard in 1932, long shining as perhaps the most brilliant member of what was before World War II one of the best economics departments in the world. As early as the 1930s he was pointing out that innovations, such as technological ones, stimulate demand for new products. As that demand is met, firms enter the market with yet more innovations. By inference, he made it clear that in periods of change, managers must transform their products to meet new conditions.[3] The most recent research on these themes urges managers to hurry up and get out of the past and into whatever the new innovation/opportunity is, so that their focus and energy are applied quickly and effectively.[4]

Schumpeter's going-in assumption is that change is constantly occurring, although there are points where bursts of change happen in rushes, such as after 1780 with steam and the Industrial Revolution, again after 1840 with what we now call the Second Industrial Revolution, and so on. That is not a bad assumption for a manager to adopt. Just because someone may not sense there is change underway does not mean it is not occurring anyway and our poor manager just has not heard about it. The change could be percolating in another industry and, thus, not appearing on some manager's industry-centric radar screen. Ice cutters of the 1800s did not develop mechanical refrigeration, nor did large mainframe computer vendors invent the personal computer.

We live in a time, however, where competent senior managers understand instinctively the issue of change and, thus, the need for reinvention from time to time. Those managers concentrate a great deal of attention on understanding who

and we did, applying the reality that made it clear value chains were useful. What is changing is that we now know they need to be dynamic and bidirectional. For that reason, you will not see a graphic of a value chain logically laid out on paper reprinted on this page, because such an illustration would suggest a static condition, exactly the wrong message to deliver.

This whole discussion, of course, is another way of saying that the customer is first. It is a practical call to arms that says processes need constant redesign, information flows change, and who performs the work of profit generation does too. Value chains also say that everyone in the workplace gets to use skills and knowledge they have acquired: process redesign and management, use of digitally-based technologies, and formation of partnerships and alliances. Supply chains transform, sometimes even becoming demand chains instead, but the idea is fairly clear. Customer-care processes now become the tip of the iceberg. But in each circumstance, business professionals focus on applying their various skills to preserve profit flows while recognizing that these flows change in content and form every few years, or even more frequently.

What we know today is that within industries, standard value chains are not as relevant in teaching managers how to make money as they were even as recently as the early 1990s. Too much is changing. Deregulation, for example, turned electric and gas utilities on their ends, radically changing by 180 degrees how they can make money and profit. Rapidly disappearing, for example, were their government-granted monopolies over specific communities where they could be the sole provider of energy; today a firm from another part of the nation can do that in many countries. In large manufacturing industries, mass customization and efficiency created new rules of engagement. In services it was the ability to provide new offerings and yet understand if they were delivered profitably. As a concept, a value chain is a useful way of thinking about one's business, because the hunt for relevant ones preserves intact an intrinsic set of core values useful from one generation of managers to another. At a minimum they remind everyone that such values are relevant all the time and should not be forgotten.

- Truck tracking and onboard computing, such as that used by Schneider, which allows the carrier to know where the truck is, who is driving, and what it is carrying

- Forecasting tools linked between supplier and user, such as that used by General Motors to ensure its suppliers of parts have the right ones arrive at the right factory at the right time

- Market demand information generated from inventory tracking systems linking point-of-sale (POS) terminals to in-store processors and to purchasers so that Walmart, for example, knows what consumers are buying and can react quickly with additional orders for replacements

- Consumer purchases on the Internet, which are directly linked back to suppliers for direct shipments to purchasers, such as is done by eBay.com

This list, it seems, is increasingly becoming more varied and extensive. Supply chain management used to be about physically moving goods around and managing inventory. Warehouse management techniques became the hot supply chain topic in the 1970s and early 1980s, although controlling and tracking inventory provided the lion's share of complicated business practices through much of the twentieth century.

If you were to discuss with IT industry long-timers what computers were used for during the past half century, they would tell you a slightly different story. They would argue that inventory control by itself was always high on any company's list of priorities, first in manufacturing and later in distribution. As firms grew in size in all industries, inventory control also became important because everyone, it seemed, had supplies on hand (inventory). The utility company had an inventory of electric lamp posts, restaurants had an inventory of frozen foods, a school an inventory of pencils, paper, and text books. Every organization had inventory. Inventories were assets that cost money and thus had to be optimized and accounted for. One IBM salesman with over 30 years of experience told me in the early 1970s that "this industry (meaning

advantage. Third, driving down the costs of making, selling, and shipping is directly possible and, in fact, is often the first benefit management receives from the use of computers. Table 5.1 lists many of the SCM processes in evidence today and in which organizational departments they reside. Each process is normally assisted by software. Every process is linked to other components of SCM and other departments by telecommunications and software tools.

Increasingly, use of information technology is stimulating activities related to the management of supply chains. The first, already mentioned, is the synchronization and optimization of supply chain processes. Second, computers are making it easier to measure and enforce compliance of participants in a process, providing anticipated levels of performance. Third, as illustrated by the processes listed in Table 5.1, the breadth of activities that could be tied together has sharply increased.

Yet we still face many challenges. Software and hardware tools keep changing, in some cases obsoleting recently acquired items. The good news is that many of these tools are not as capital-intensive as in previous decades because often they are highly dispersed small components (e.g., software, PCs, and hand-held units), linked together through wireless or telephone lines to software and databases on existing mainframe computers, and in the future they may be accessed on a transaction basis through ASPs. In other instances, parts of the supply chain are being managed by partners and allies using their own telecommunications and computer systems. This means a manager can change the structure of a supply chain a great deal faster today than ten or twenty years ago.

An important challenge is dealing with the fact that as one tightens up the supply chain, he or she is forced to do three things well. First, the manager must develop a clear idea of what the supply chain has to do and why. That includes understanding expectations and being able to measure them. This effort causes a manager to organize and do things fundamentally differently than might have been the case even a decade ago. Look at how Dell Computers, for example, taught its industry that it could provide personal computers and not own a factory or a store! Second, organizations need to be able to

use their computers effectively to perform tasks involved in a supply chain, but also to draw from those systems information and insights about what is happening within the supply chain's processes. This allows a manager to change a product mix or the timing of a delivery, identify areas of cost control, and so forth. Third, a manager must be prepared to change frequently and quickly how business functions. This third duty is the one executives often find the most difficult to perform. There are many obvious barriers to change. These include insufficient desire to do the hard work, measurements and incentives that motivate individuals to leave things as they are, danger to one's political power or career, lack of appreciation for what really needs to change, and fear of risk, particularly the concern over potential lost revenue or increased surprise costs. Yet, at the end of the day, these challenges must be overcome.

The good news is that over the past half century managers have injected information technology into their supply chains without knowing that this was what they were doing—automating major portions of their supply chains—until we began to see whole bodies of linked activities as SCM by the early 1990s. Today inventory control with computers is a very familiar area of expertise found in almost any company. Telecommunications and use of personal computers, even hand-held units, is now a widely understood body of technology. POS and scanning technologies are as well understood in manufacturing as they are by retail and distribution firms. However, wireless technologies, really the basis of a new telecommunications industry first evident in the second half of the 1990s, represent a frontier of unknowns. New products and price/performance levels are just emerging. Governments are regulating and deregulating wireless activities as you read this book. New applications are only just now being realized, while old wire-based ones are being replaced with wireless systems. All of this is going on around the world, in poor countries in Africa and in those East Asian and northern European states with the highest standards of living on our planet.

One challenge we face is an inadequate supply of best practices in the world of SCM and value chains. The business press, particularly in North America, has sharply increased its

they have always been keys to success in earlier periods of transformation and are the behaviors those currently thriving in the Information Age are displaying.

Increasingly, the knowledge needed will not be in one person's head. In the case of what types of telecommunications and computing to use, a number of experts already have to be in constant dialogue with managers and users of the supply chain. You can expect to see more of that kind of interaction in the future. That is why, for example, many companies are creating supply chain councils and task forces that are, in effect, permanent and extend beyond their enterprises. You can even see supply chain executives appointed, charged with responsibility for lashing together all the players, many of whom are experts in information technology and telecommunications, not just simply manufacturing and warehouse gurus.

This requirement of lashing together parts of an organization raises the inevitable question of how high in an organization the key decision maker has to be. Ironically, when in the 1970s Peter F. Drucker discussed the issue of where to place decision making in any organization, he used the example of inventory control (precursor to supply chains) as the point at which he wanted to teach his readers.[9] The moral is clear: While many things are changing, some principles of sound management do not.

SOME REALITIES

The most pervasive trend in recent years has been the integration of SCM with the Internet and other forms of information technology. This integrative activity has reached out to every form of digital technology available to organizations, even stimulating the development of new technical tools in the process. It took management very little time to realize the strategic and operational importance of weaving technology into its supply chains. The returns came fast and furious, making it easy to conclude that a path to new value chains is the transformation of one's supply chain. That insight suggests

and innovation is *Business Cycles: A Theoretical, Historical, and Statistical Analysis of the Capitalist Process* (New York: McGraw-Hill, 1939), subsequently reprinted in a variety of editions.

4. For an excellent introduction, see James M. Utterback, *Mastering the Dynamics of Innovation: How Companies Can Seize Opportunities in the Face of Technological Change* (Boston: Harvard Business School Press, 1994), especially pp. 189–213.

5. This best practice is the subject of an entire book, James W. Cortada and Thomas S. Hargraves (eds.), *Into the Networked Age: How IBM and Other Firms Are Getting There Now* (New York: Oxford University Press, 1999).

6. The logic was simple. If software could help someone reduce the amount of on-hand inventory that they needed by just several percentage points, the cash flow savings would more than offset the cost of the computer system. Since everyone felt that they had several percentage points of too much inventory, the justification was seductive. The IBM salesman who experienced the initial surge in the installation of computers in the United States in the late 1950s through the 1970s was Gus Kane.

7. For a recent collection of such materials, see John A. Woods and the National Association of Purchasing Management (eds.), *The Purchasing and Supply Yearbook* (New York: McGraw-Hill, 2000).

8. It was Napoleon Bonaparte who called out the value of supply chain management when he said, "An army marches on its stomach." Every major military force since his time has focused on making sure soldiers and sailors had food, weapons, ammunition, and the other inventories of war.

9. Peter F. Drucker, *Management: Tasks, Responsibilities, Practices* (New York: Harper & Row, 1973), 544, 545.

CHOOSING A FUTURE FOR YOUR COMPANY

Nobody could make a greater mistake than to do nothing because he could do only a little.

EDMUND BURKE

The ultimate dream of all managers is to be master of one's own destiny. Employees share this same aspiration. If this could be achieved, managers, together with their teams of employees and business partners, would ensure the success of their own companies, careers, and bank accounts. Their firms would be large, profitable, own a great deal of market share, and be revered as national assets. Scholars and newspaper reporters would interview them to uncover their "secrets of success," writing articles and books about them. But this need not be just a dream or wishful thinking; it happens to some people and their companies. Just since World War II, using the American experience as an example, we can point to Jack Welch and GE, Thomas Watson, Jr., and IBM, Lee Iacocca and Chrysler, and to Bill Gates and Microsoft. Among the hot Internet and other IT firms, new icons are emerging all the time:

THE FUTURE OF THE BUSINESS ENTERPRISE

As the amount of change in the economies of the world became increasingly evident, beginning in the early 1980s, the amount of speculation about the future of the business enterprise increased. Walk into any bookstore in London, New York, Tokyo, or Rio de Janeiro and you will see dozens of books for sale about how to manage corporations in the Age of Information or in the Internet World. Peter F. Drucker even got in on the act with his wonderful book, *Managing in Turbulent Times* and later with others on the same theme. The future is an important topic and its significance should not be minimized. But forecasts have varied enormously in vision and perspective; most have been based on speculation, while a few have attempted to take existing trends and project them out in time. The demographers have been the best at doing this, which is why I relied on their work in some of the earlier chapters of this book.

We are left, however, with the problem of speculation, which on the one hand makes for good book sales, but on the other leaves us just with speculation, guesses about the future. What we do know is that managers have the capability of forging part of their future through design, just like some of the previously mentioned business executives did. If, for example, a person wanted to sell goods through retail outlets, that individual would form an enterprise with storefronts. Another, who concludes that the best way to sell goods is through the Internet, would not have an organization populated with stores, just a room full of computers and telephone operators. So, the first conclusion we can reach about the future of the business enterprise is that a team of managers and employees does have a strong influence over the future characteristics of its firm. This is so much the case that we do not have to present that conclusion as a hypothesis; history teaches us that we can influence future events.

A second stake we can put in the ground is our knowledge today that it does make sense to formulate a vision and an

prise. For example, IBM sells and delivers large computers to customers while it uses dealers to sell personal computers, and is building a services business that is larger than most hardware and software firms in the IT industry. Within IBM, nearly a third of its business comes from services, which has a principal-based consulting structure, complete with its own culture, metrics, values, and ways of doing business, all created in less than a decade.[2] But, in the final analysis, every existing enterprise exists with one foot in the past and another in the future, with the present a mixture of the two in transition.

In their study, *Built to Last*, Collins and Porras pointed out what experienced senior executives have long understood, that evolution is normally incremental and constantly occurring. Exceptions are the stuff of history: major downturns in business, causing downsizing and restructuring, or radical technological changes disrupting routine sources of revenue and profit. The invention of the refrigerator in the United States wiped out New England ice cutters, the PC just about killed mini-computers, and a successful electric car could do serious damage to the oil industry. But these are the exceptions, despite the enormous hype to the contrary. What makes change seem dramatic is the fact that it occurs continuously and every industry is involved in it, as suggested in Chapter One. Incremental change is cumulative in effect, however, which is why one can look back and see that over time so much had evolved.

From the perspective of anyone working in business, therefore, understanding the levers of change—such as technology, telecommunications, new management fads, deconstruction of markets and industries—has the greatest effect if they are selected as tools to facilitate change. What the history of business teaches us is that change occurs and employees at all levels of an organization must pick what tools to use. But they make the changes.

Making changes based on an understanding of levers of transformation stands in sharp contrast to the way change is normally described. One usually reads articles and books that

maintained their identity as suppliers of technology.[3] This perspective is not to be confused with what happens to users of technology, that is, those who acquire electronics, computers, and chemicals. Their use of these products causes them to change the construct of their firms and industry borders as they too pursue their own paths of learning and economic advantage. The cross-industry changes we are currently witnessing with desegregation of some industries, others affected by the Internet of course, injects a certain amount of anxiety and uncertainty about the lessons of time. But Chandler's observations are not to be ignored because some industry-centric skills are profound and effective, such as how the pharmaceuticals know how to develop new drugs and bring them to market.

Given these several realities, it becomes more important to understand how to make changes in the future of organizations because we know that form often follows function. Historians of business have confirmed repeatedly that investments in technology, management practices, and organizations must be made in a coordinated manner to be effective. Firms and industries learn how to do this for better or for worse. But they do it. Best practices in this arena do not really exist about what the end product is, but rather how to reach it. Experience, experimentation, and research suggest nine sets of activities and attitudes that affect a firm's future. Experience would suggest that all nine are in play in the mind and actions of the good manager.

1. *Building some assumptions on which managers are willing to bet their future.* Often, their bet is on an emerging technology, such as the Internet: "We will need to use the Internet as our major channel of distribution within five years."
2. *Creating a set of objectives that one is willing to organize around.* For example, a state governor might say, "We will have to educate 50 percent more students in a decade at the same cost as we do today; little inflation in budgets may be affordable." That was an objective

activities of the 1980s, learned from Japanese quality experts, was the value of integrating changes in process, people, technology, and policies. The tools and techniques of that experience provide the nuts-and-bolts "down in the trenches" list of activities that gives any change tangible reality.

6. *Accepting the reality that changes come in many forms and at various speeds, all simultaneously.* A colleague and I took a hard look at the nature of change in the world of IT in the mid-1990s and discovered that computing does not just change in any general sense. Rather, specific changes occur simultaneously within an organization. We found that PCs were being replaced every one to two years, operating systems for these machines at least once every year. Large applications sitting on mainframes, on the other hand, had many subtle changes over the years (e.g., went to database, from batch to online, from terminals to PCs) and often remained in use for over twenty years.[6] A similar phenomenon of multiple rates of change provides the confusion and dichotomies all managers and their staffs face today, whether in how marketing is done or how computers are deployed.

7. *Recognizing that consequences last much longer than is generally acknowledged.* Since this book is about managing and working in the Age of Information, IT examples illustrate the point. In the period 1961–1964, all the major computer vendors around the world made a series of decisions about the architecture of the operating systems that would control computer systems. Some forty years later, these decisions were still in force because the operating systems were essentially very similar to those of the mid-1960s. The Y2K problem is another example; the decisions that led to the problem were made in the 1950s! IBM's decision to use an open architecture for PCs, a decision made in 1980, led to the creation of a massive PC industry and to Microsoft. Neither decision looks like it will be reversed

see that these patterns and their related issues and controversies were alive and well then. The best managers figure out how much to delegate, what skills to invest in, and how much top down control is necessary to ensure that the entire organization is headed in a direction that reflects senior management's will and what the enterprise knows collectively will work in the immediate future.

Before I continue this discussion, let me point out that the extensive use of the pronoun *you* in the preceding list is by design because given the way we use technology, especially e-mail, and the increased delegation of authority lower in organizations means that more managers and nonmanagers than ever have a profound influence on the direction taken by any enterprise. It is another way of pointing a finger directly at those who are saying grace over the future of their firms, *you*.

In the final analysis, change occurs, leading to new futures for any firm. But these changes are complex, occur at various speeds, and reside simultaneously with familiar forms. One's company still has basic activities from one decade to another: accounting, marketing, legal, communications, manufacturing, distribution, service, sales, and so forth. Changes within these occur and are subject to much debate and forecasting. Yet it is at the micro-level (e.g., within a process or function) that people are best directed in worrying about what the future of the enterprise might be. How they do that is the subject of our next two discussions, one about trends, the other on how management practices change.

MAKING TRENDS WORK FOR THE FIRM

Like the Greek politicos, generals, and merchants of ancient times going to their temples to see what the gods had to say, managers today recognize that often success involves doing the right things at the right time. Scenario planning in strategy development is a modern day attempt to qualify the future so that one could be at the right place at the right time.

tar-fighting mouthwashes for the parents). They do that for most of their products already, a key reason why this firm has been so successful for so many decades.

Demographic data is another good source of trends. This is more than just understanding how many people are of what ages or where they live. The subject has been extended to such a level of detail as to be a science in business, documenting spending habits of consumers, documenting and correlating economic behavior by age group, educational level, religion, and ethnic background, even by what one charges to their credit cards. But it all comes back to basics, and demographics is no exception. All the people who will be twenty years old in fifteen years have already been born. We can, therefore, begin following the changing trend in clothing that the change in sizes—due to normal growth—will cause, and also begin forecasting the trend going forward through various grades in school and into careers later.

Trends also have their limits, a reality often overlooked by both prognosticators and managers eager for a view of the future. A trend cannot tell you exactly how much toothpaste we really will use next year, nor indicate what university a child of mine will attend, where toothpaste will be sold, nor whether that child will continue the same hygienic habits imposed on them at home by my wife. A child might change brands of toothpaste or go live in another country where our currently used brand of toothpaste is not available. The manufacturer could run into an unpredicted problem due to some bad chemical accident like Coca-Cola ran into in Western Europe in 1999, thereby causing customers to switch to other products. Then, there are the inevitable natural disasters— earthquakes, bad weather, floods, and so forth—to deal with, not to mention political conditions, which business managers usually ignore, but which come along too, such as revolutions, ethnic unrest, or significant changes in democratically elected political parties.

We must, therefore, recognize the limits of trends. They are useful up to a certain point. Now, the reason for this little dissertation on trends is because we live in an age in which

mately, the use of trends boils down to what an individual believes will be the case. After the consultants, and after the industry reports and prognostications, a manager is left alone with only his or her mind for counsel. It is at that point that opinions have to be formalized, decisions taken, necks stuck out.

Is there some help, some possible trends that we can count on without having to read 15 more chapters to understand? With apologies to those who want a detailed defense of them, here is my quick list of some useful trends upon which to base some strategic and tactical agendas.

Skills and knowledge must change and grow constantly to remain current and competitive. This means that as managers and employees we must always have formal programs in place for the development of individuals, ourselves and those with whom we work. Interestingly, experience in recent years demonstrates that employees are willing to acquire new skills, regardless of whether their employers are willing or able to pay them more for the increased productivity generated by these improved skills.

Fact-based decision making will increase as management and the practice of business become more "scientific," with a greater reliance on survey results and the analytical byproducts of consulting projects. Process management and knowledge management practices simply are encouraging the use of more data as input to decisions. We can, therefore, expect more of that in the years to come.

As businesses become more international, increase the IT content of their work, and add more services (if originally in manufacturing), the kinds of people who are members of a firm will be more varied. This mix in education and experience will bring a richer diversity of perspectives to a business. Managers will have to find ways to leverage what appears to be a very positive trend, perhaps along with the increased reliance on research and data, to run an enterprise.

We already know that there will be more process-centric, IT-laden work processes, the subject of much discussion in this book. However, the significant implication here is that

Managers who have worked throughout the 1980s and 1990s have learned that as their profession became more disciplined, they had to become continuous students of their trade. Many went back to graduate school in executive MBA programs, while hundreds of thousands became avid readers of business books and magazines. They are the ones that account for the fact that the number of new business books and magazines published and sold throughout the world (both on paper and online) has been increasing steadily throughout this period. So change begets more demand for information, hence the need to spend time learning new things.

Given these various trends, is it possible to settle on a short list of basics that do not change? It turns out the answer is yes.

NATURE OF MANAGEMENT PRACTICES

Economists and business management experts have moved toward a consensus on some essential truths. After all the studies, downsizing initiatives, publications, and fads of the last two decades of the twentieth century, some basic lessons remain to carry forward. Ironically, while much has been learned that is new and valuable, we have yet to see a major consolidation and integration of these insights. Part of the reason this has not happened is that we are still experiencing so many changes in all professions in business, including in management. But part of the reason also lies with consultants and professors not taking the bold step of cataloging what we know. It is possible to create a short list, and there is empirical evidence to back every line item on it. Here are a few things to start you thinking about management and leadership.

First, the most successful companies now understand the true value and application of best practices. What makes these companies most effective is that a collection of best practices is routinely implemented. These managers recognize that life is holistic, and so are good management practices. It is not enough to be outstanding in one process, but rather in many

work is the use of downsizing to swap out employees with the wrong skills for those that have the experience and knowledge necessary to implement a new business strategy. The short term benefits of downsizing lie primarily in reducing costs to stop the hemorrhaging of the balance sheet. For skilled employees, downsizing sends them to other firms where their skills, experience, and interests are in more demand.

Fifth, the most productive R&D is that undertaken by the private sector in support of specific product improvements and innovations. These are effective because the best companies do this in response to market demands. Economist Richard K. Lester argues that analyzing and developing alternatives work well when the market is best understood. If you have to create a new outcome, then interpreting the potential of a new product or technology represents a more effective approach to R&D, a situation many in business often face with technology-based products. The interpretive approach places greater value on dealing with ongoing ambiguity in the market, the analytical calls for closure in the sense of developing, building, and selling products, then moving on to the next projects.[8]

Sixth, listening to the voice of the customer through an organized process—sense and response to real market conditions—provides very useful indicators of where a firm should direct its activities. Analyzing patterns of contact by customers with organizations has become a rapidly expanding new application of computers, providing significant marketing data. Thus, for example, when a customer attempts to buy a PC from a vendor over the Internet, the supplier can track what options people look at and adopt or reject. Types of telephone queries offer additional insights. These kinds of data can be tabulated neatly by computers and presented to management in forms that allow them to take action indicated by patterns of buyer behavior. The same applies to watching consumer behavior in stores.

Seventh, just listening to the voice of the customer can also be a bad practice. Customers only know what they know, what they are familiar with. They do not always know what a firm is capable of doing. Employees often know what the

mium in that brave new world, which we are entering, is the same as it was in that of the Second Industrial Revolution of the nineteenth and twentieth centuries: acquisition and use of knowledge and, hence, leveraging the elements that make up knowledge and wisdom, experience and information.

Dertouzos makes an important distinction from what we frequently read, particularly in the United States and in Western Europe. For a half century we have routinely been inundated with arguments that our lives will be filled with computer chips, robots will do our bidding, and machines will take over much work. The implication underpinning such messages is that there exists a technological determinism hard at work, as if the hand of God was robotic, leaving us little choice in deciding what to do. However, and despite some abuses in the use of technologies of various types or negative consequences we see from time-to-time, people always had choices. Technologies do not come into play unless someone elects to use them. Choices are always conditioned, however, by knowledgeable innovation. The eternal footrace all businesses participate in—competition—is increasingly won or lost based on the ability to innovate, to stay close to markets, and to exploit some new piece of knowledge or technology just a little faster than the next firm. This is an applications view of the world. That is the future, a world characterized by people applying information to work, not work being taken over by computers.

The distinction is subtle but important. By thinking in terms of information needed to do work, we force ourselves to make technology subservient to our needs. We rely more or less on computers to the extent that these machines provide more or less, better or poorer information relevant to what people do. Not all businesses are warehouses filled with computers and telephone lines. Some industries need to use this technology more than others but the flip side is also true: Some industries need to use such technology less frequently than others. Why? Follow the flow of information, the volume of its consumption, the nature of its use, the speed and cost of its movement, and you will find the answer. A cement factory uses computers, but far fewer than an oil refinery. Why? Both

Because so many changes are occurring so fast, and particularly now as a result of the Internet, we will have to spend a greater percentage of our time learning and keeping up-to-date than might have been the case two decades ago. As changes occur, so too does the requirement for new information, experience, and knowledge. That is why book and magazine publishers will continue to be useful as sources of information to help keep us current. Change and currency in turn create new churn, additional change, and generate new knowledge, because good managers apply what they learn for economic benefit. We pay managers to do this. Many managers already recognize that an important part of their work is to be students of their work and profession, having the inquisitive qualities of a researcher, while displaying the impatience and courage of an entrepreneur.

Those last two qualities are always at a premium during periods of change such as the one we are moving through to some as yet undefined future. One theory holds that eventually we will come to some steady state, where knowledge and experience stabilize for some period of time. The two previous industrial revolutions, however, offer evidence that if such a steady state exists, it does so for a very short period of time, and unevenly from one sector of the economy to another. Reality is that the transition from one state to another takes multiple decades, and forecasters never have seen the end as it really came to be. We know that we are in transition to a new future, which places a premium on handling ambiguity well. Ambiguity for a manager is both a danger and an opportunity. Those in a stable enterprise see it as a threat, those with less investment in the past as an opportunity. The competitive edge goes to those who act more as knowledge leaders than as experts in technology.

At both strategic and tactical levels, managers are learning how to function in an "Information Marketplace" (Dertouzos' apt phrase for it). Information has economic value:

- The mailing list that can be sold
- The information that leads to products customers want
- The data that leads to lower costs of doing business

Particularly over the last half century, managers have been finding new ways to use computers to track activities, and in the process fundamentally shifted from measuring periodic activities (e.g., on a weekly or monthly basis) to real-time and ongoing (by the second or minute). While digital computers have come into their own, we have evolved to the point of favoring an analog view of data. We now want information and measurements on what is happening right now. It seems that every machine of any large size, and all large computer-based applications, are tracking and reporting something that is then used by operators and users to determine how next to run a machine or take some other action.

Beginning in the 1920s, although with some primitive thinking as far back as the 1860s and 1870s, managers have developed a whole body of knowledge about how to look at activities as processes, complete with best practices and favorite measurements. In recent years, advocates of process management have been lionized for adding new practices to the kits of all good managers (Joseph Juran, W. Edwards Deming, Walter Shewhart, and Kaoru Ishikawa).

Use of statistics as applied in business became one of the most important intellectual and knowledge-based innovations of the twentieth century in the field of business practices. Already emerging as a branch of mathematics in the 1800s, solidified into a body of knowledge by the end of World War I, statistics came into business by the mid-1920s. Operations management techniques emerged by the end of World War II, and statistical process control (SPC) methods for measuring processes evolved at the same time as process management came into its own. Today, I cannot imagine operating a business process without a broad range of measurements to understand the effectiveness and nature of its performance. If the quality management movement (if we can call it a movement) taught us anything, it was (a) know thy customer's thoughts and desires while assuming nothing without questioning, and (b) measure everything important. The latter became increasingly possible as we moved through the second half of the twentieth century, largely because of computers, advances in cost accounting techniques and, simultaneously, statistical process control. Next, computers came along, facilitating the further expansion of these two approaches to measurements during the 1950s and 1960s. As a consequence of new ways of looking at numbers, and the application of a broad range of measuring instruments and computers, various approaches emerged for the application of accounting and SPC in management around the world. Each has its adherents and detractors. However, several approaches to the use of measurements are now widely used, often in combination, and they are used in organizations that are squarely in the Information Age and in others rooted in the Second Industrial Age. The most popular are:

- Activity-based costing (ABC)
- Balanced score cards
- Integrated hierarchies of measures (often pyramidlike)
- Report cards

Other "systems" exist but most can be traced back to these four approaches. All four are normally continuous and, as the century progressed, were increasingly integrated into a matrix of measures in support of an organization's management team. Today, many people across all industries and in most professions are generally familiar with one or more of these approaches. Missing from the list are financial measures, such as ROI, E/R ratios, and so forth, left out on purpose because they are tools and techniques for forming opinions about situations and opportunities/risks, while the four approaches listed represent strategies for measuring performance of processes and people. We moved from simply creating measurement techniques to measure results (1840s–1930s) to implementing measures that identified how activities were aligned with the objectives of the organization (1950s–1980s). Today a combination of all strategies is most often in evidence, and we are still learning more about the strengths and weaknesses of each approach.[12]

Activity-based costing, known more familiarly to a generation of managers simply as ABC, has taken over three decades to make it into the mainstream of accounting practices, and

system because it allows you to clarify and translate vision and strategy into action, gain feedback, plan and set targets, and communicate. This method of measuring performance has clearly become the winner over all the other available measurement systems introduced over the past quarter century. It is simple to understand, relatively easy to implement because it often relies on existing bodies of information, and can be used both to lead to action and to define problems.

Integrated hierarchies of measures represent another approach that is almost as popular, but with the great advantage in that it provides another level of detail normally not available through balanced score cards. Often depicted as pyramids, with various layers of measures from transaction-based unit counts at the bottom to measures of strategic results, these also rely extensively on measures coming out of process management. They can include an assortment of metrics on transactions, defects, customer interactions, costs by unit, profits, types of activities, and so forth. The key is understanding what types of activities affect some other action or measure because managers tend to be very wary of altering a measure without first understanding potential unintended consequences. These kinds of metrics are great for exploring cause and effect. For example, a user learns that waste affects productivity measures negatively, while increasing cycle time. On the other hand, higher or lower reliability influences the amount of waste and poor/better quality. Reliability, quality, and waste influence how much cycle time is involved with a particular activity or process (and its costs), while cycle time affects productivity, flexibility, and customer satisfaction. The point is, new lessons are constantly being learned about the cause and effect of measured activities, giving managers increased insight into how to improve the performance of specific or overall activities and organizations.[14]

Finally, a new set of measures called report cards has recently arrived. Like the other families of reports, this too can be generated by collecting bodies of information, often housed in computers, to provide a composite picture of how an organization is doing. Like a student's report card, it can provide grades or performance statistics on one page (or

about the future, the most fundamental way of directing an organization toward it is by telling stories that reflect the values of the organization. Leaders and managers share a common set of values with their colleagues and employees, coming very close to the key point of my book: that we must manage in an environment rooted in the past and yet stepping forward into a new future.[15]

The innovative quality in us is what is required to make the transition. It is why there is so much emphasis today on innovation. But what Gardner found when he looked at many examples of innovative leadership was that the whole process boiled down to forming a confident opinion about where to go, sharing that view in ways that resonate with the experiences and values of an organization to get buy-in, and following up by the application of normal management practices to implement the plan. It sounds simple, but as I have argued all through this book, focusing on the basics of time-honored sound management and business practices is going to be the key to success as we move forward. That the actual tasks will often be complicated and that ambiguity and uncertainty will remain a constant feature of our environment are undeniable. But remaining calm, confident, and focused in the face of all these circumstances works, just as it has in prior times of significant change. Peter Drucker, in his 89th year of life, made a similar point, arguing at length that the basics of management are not changing, only some of the tasks managers perform.[16]

The combination of sound management practices, coupled to a view of where to take a department or a firm, remains crucial in these times. While we will continue to be bombarded with new technologies, tools, methods, techniques, and best practices, they are, at the end of the day, just tools. We can choose to use them or not.

What is very obvious, however, is that the choice of tools will be profoundly influenced by the circumstances described in this book. There is no doubt, for example, that e-business approaches will profoundly change the tasks of workers as much activity is performed with the use of digital tools, and as a great deal of information is collected, analyzed, and moved

cuting with a growing body of management and business practices fit for the Information Age. My argument in this book is that the challenge we face is to operate businesses in a world that has one foot in the Industrial Age and another in the Information Age. That is not an easy thing to do, but many of the practices that applied well in the later stages of the Industrial Age will facilitate our rapid migration to the Information Age. Understanding what changes, and how transformation occurs, offers you and I a path to future success.

ENDNOTES

1. James C. Collins and Jerry I. Porras, *Built to Last* (New York: HarperBusiness, 1994).

2. Principal-based management means that the person who sells a service also performs some of the work just sold. This is the classic business model for consulting organizations.

3. Alfred D. Chandler, Jr., study forthcoming.

4. Of the many books written by Charles Handy, the one that perhaps most of all introduced his ideas to management and influenced their thinking the most is *The Age of Unreason* (Boston: Harvard Business School Press, 1989).

5. This is an industry that clearly demonstrates my argument that managers have a great say in what their future will be. In the United States, banks agitated for regulatory permission to sell insurance and financial products, such as stocks, which had not been allowed in the U.S. since the Great Depression of the 1930s. In November 1999, the American government passed a law making it possible for banks to offer these products. The change was a direct result of American executives agitating for this new future, thereby joining banks in many other countries that had already arrived at their future, one in which they could sell insurance and financial products.

6. Michael Albrecht and James W. Cortada, "Optimizing Investments in Information Technology," *National Productivity Review* (Summer 1998): 53–61.

7. Richard K. Lester, *The Productive Edge* (New York: W.W. Norton and Company, 1998): 320.

ON KEEPING CURRENT: A STRATEGY AND SOME USEFUL READING

A fool can learn from his own experience, the wise learn from the experiences of others.

DEMOCRITUS

If you read this book, then you know what is coming. It should be clear that understanding how the world operates and the changes it undergoes remains essential to your professional success. It is also essential to the survival of the organizations in which you work. The process of keeping current, of learning from your experience and studies, is constant at both the personal and institutional levels. But this short essay is less about the organization and more about the individual. Whether a CEO of a large company or a freshly minted university graduate, the lessons of the wise and those who do well in periods of change remain as they always have, lessons of timeless quality. The strategy is simple to describe, but like a good diet, one that we must get in the habit of practicing. The discussion following is broken into two pieces: the practice and some great reading.

tion of use to you. About a half dozen well-chosen ones from *outside* your organization should do the trick.

Third, expand your circle of friends, associates, and people you meet to include those in other industries and organizations. Ask them constantly what they are doing, where their organizations are headed, what new initiatives they are taking, and why. Connections begin to pop up all the time, but you have to be curious.

SOME GREAT READING

Since much of the best thinking about management and work in the Information Age is best explained these days in books, what might be a good reading list? Everyone has their own favorites, these are mine that I have found thoughtful and relevant. I do not think it unreasonable to expect that eventually you would have read most of these if you are serious about deeply understanding the world you are working in today.

On the role of management, almost everyone begins with Peter F. Drucker. His latest book, *Management Challenges for the 21st Century* (New York: HarperBusiness, 1999), distills many of the key elements of management in contemporary terms and is a very quick read. The number of great books available on leadership is staggering, but I want to suggest one written by a scientist of the mind, rather than by a business professor: *Leading Minds: An Anatomy of Leadership* (New York: HarperBusiness, 1995), by Howard Gardner, in which he describes what leaders do who come from many walks of life. Read one of his books and you will want to find others (he has published about 15).

A central element of today's work mantra is the voice of the customer, and on that topic there are also hundreds of books, many of them superficial. However, two are essential, maybe even perfect. For over two decades, a cultural anthropologist, Paco Underhill, has studied how people buy and sell, summarizing his fascinating discoveries in a short, well-written book: *Why We Buy: The Science of Shopping,* by Paco

ert S. Kaplan and David P. Norton took their notion of the Balanced Scorecard and wrote a book explaining all its attributes and how to implement it in *The Balanced Scorecard* (Boston: Harvard Business School Press, 1996). For an effective overview of other measurements systems, there is nothing better than *Measure Up! Yardsticks for Continuous Improvement,* by Richard L. Lynch and Kelvin F. Cross (Oxford: Blackwell, 1991).

Technology has become the subject of many excellent books that read well and are informative for people at all levels of an organization. James M. Utterback, in *Mastering the Dynamics of Innovation* (Boston: Harvard Business School Press, 1994), combines historical case studies and contemporary experiences to describe how to best leverage technologies in general, not just IT. For the dark side of that story with lessons learned, see Clayton M. Christensen's well received book, *The Innovator's Dilemma: When New Technologies Cause Great Firms to Fail* (Boston: Harvard Business School, 1997).

What should you read about information technology? Begin with Carl Shapiro and Hal R. Varian, who, in *Information Rules: A Strategic Guide to the Network Economy* (Boston: Harvard Business School, 1999), show how fundamental business practices are applied in a networked era. Then, read a book by Philip Evans and Thomas S. Wurster, *Blown to Bits: How the New Economics of Information Transforms Strategy* (Boston: Harvard Business School Press, 2000) which, like the earlier book, discusses strategy. Since IT has to provide continuous improvement in operations, there is my tactical description of how that is done, James W. Cortada, *Best Practices in Information Technology: How Corporations Get the Most Value from Exploiting Their Digital Investments* (Upper Saddle River, N.J.: Prentice Hall PTR, 1998).

The bible on knowledge management was written by Laurence Prusak. *Working Knowledge* (Boston: Harvard Business School Press, 1997) provides a clear explanation of the rationale and use of KM. For a more argumentative yet stimulating book on information technology and KM, there is Thomas H. Davenport's *Information Ecology: Mastering the Information*

S. Landes, *The Wealth and Poverty of Nations: Why Some Are So Rich and Some So Poor* (New York: W.W. Norton, 1998); it may be the best history book you will have read in a long time, covering the entire sweep of human history and the effects of the environment and economy on nations. Joel Mokyr has written on how technology affected economic prosperity in *The Lever of Riches: Technological Creativity and Economic Progress* (New York: Oxford University Press, 1990). While a very long book, and in some parts tough reading, David Hackett Fischer's *The Great Wave: Price Revolutions and the Rhythm of History* (New York: Oxford University Press, 1996) is the ultimate word on historical economic waves and trends. Many of his appendices are excellent short tutorials on waves and price patterns; at a minimum you should read some of those. The classic work on the history of corporations and management remains the remarkable book by the father of business history, Alfred D. Chandler, Jr., *The Visible Hand: The Managerial Revolution in American Business* (Cambridge, Mass.: Harvard University Press, 1977). Once you have read a book by Chandler you will want to read others by him.

Curious about the Internet or about the history of computing? The hands down best history of the Internet is by Janet Abbate, *Inventing the Internet* (Cambridge, Mass.: MIT Press, 1999). You will learn that there is more to technology than technology; institutional politics and objectives are at least as important as physics and technologies in determining how telecommunications and computers evolved. A classic account of the PC is by Paul Freiberger and Michael Swaine, *Fire in the Valley: The Making of the Personal Computer* (New York: McGraw-Hill, 2000, 2nd edition). For a book that combines sociology, business, and a little history about the Internet, see the very wise and readable Andrew L. Shapiro, *The Control Revolution* (New York: Public Affairs, 1999). Finally, for a major history of the role of information in the United States, a book designed for both the general public and those in business, and written by historians, consultants and business professors, see Alfred D. Chandler, Jr., and James W. Cortada (eds.), *A Nation Transformed by Information: How Informa-*

INDEX

U.S. taxes and, 30
  trading hubs, 181
  uniqueness of, 145-148
Intranets, 143
Inventory, modern control role, 195-196
  SCM reduces, 177, 178
Ishikawa, Kaoru, 229
ITT, lessons learned by, 56

J

Japan, dominance in consumer
    electronics, 55
Juran, Joseph, 210, 229
  advocated process management, 72

K

Kaplan, Robert S., popularized
    scorecards, 232
Kearns, David T., 208
Knowledge, value of, 224-228
Knowledge management, bad practices,
    109-110
  best practices, 120-131
  business role of, 51-89
  e-business role, 116-120
  how to implement, 104-106, 108-
    115
  how transforms commerce, 65-70;
    process management and,
    73
  reasons for, 110-111
Knowledge workers, described, 95-131;
    effectiveness of, 102-110;
    in USA, 5-6
  origins of, 100-103

L

L.L. Bean, on the Net, 142
Labor, content of products reducing,
    126
  productivity, 19
Land's End, use of computers by, 170
Leadership, 224-228

in Information Age, 234-237
  knowledge management and, 107
Learnings, effect on industries, 54-55
Lester, Richard K., ideas of, 223
Levi Strauss, on the Net, 141
Levitt, Theodore, ideas of, 57
Linz, Juan J., on democracy, 40
Lotus Notes, 66, 185
  knowledge management tool, 106
Lycos, 18

M

Machlup, Fritz, xx
  on information economy, 4
Management, changing role of, 87-90,
    123-124
  challenges in Information Age, 45-
    47
  evolves into profession, 52-54
  knowledge management and, 64-70
  modern tasks of, 125-130
  nature of, 221-224
  of supply chains, 199
  on managing Internet, 145-146
  on sharing responsibilities, 74
Markets, access to, 149-150
  entry and exit using knowledge
    management, 122
Marketspace, described, 153-154
Mass customization, role of, 25-26
McDonald's, core competency of, 57-58
McNealy, Scott, 206
Measurements, trends in, 228-235
Mercedes-Benz, 214
  IT competencies of, 62
Mergers and acquisitions (M&As),
    affected by technology,
    181-182
  trends, 17
Microsoft, 13, 187, 191, 213
  acquisition strategy of, 59
  hires knowledge workers, 102
  value of knowledge at, 104
  value of stock, 11
  working conditions at, 123